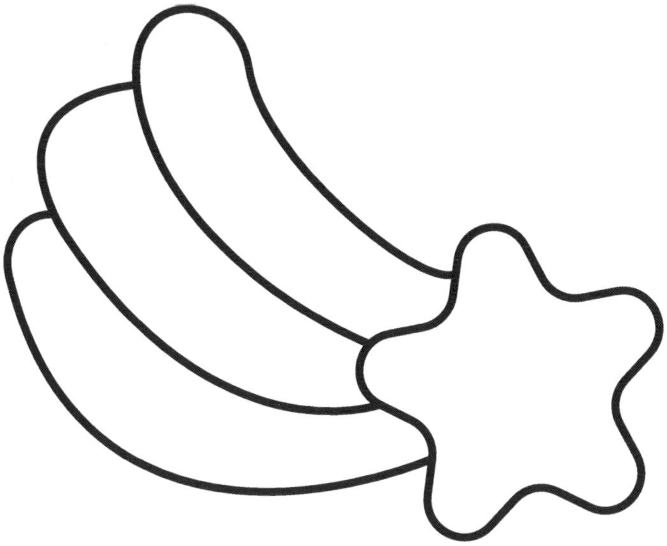

THIS BOOK BELONGS TO:

_ _ _ _ _ _ _ _ _ _ _ _ _ _ _ _ _ _ _ _

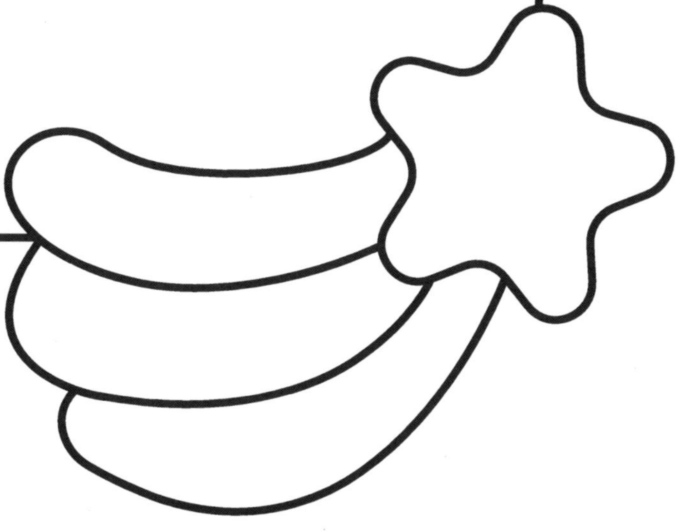

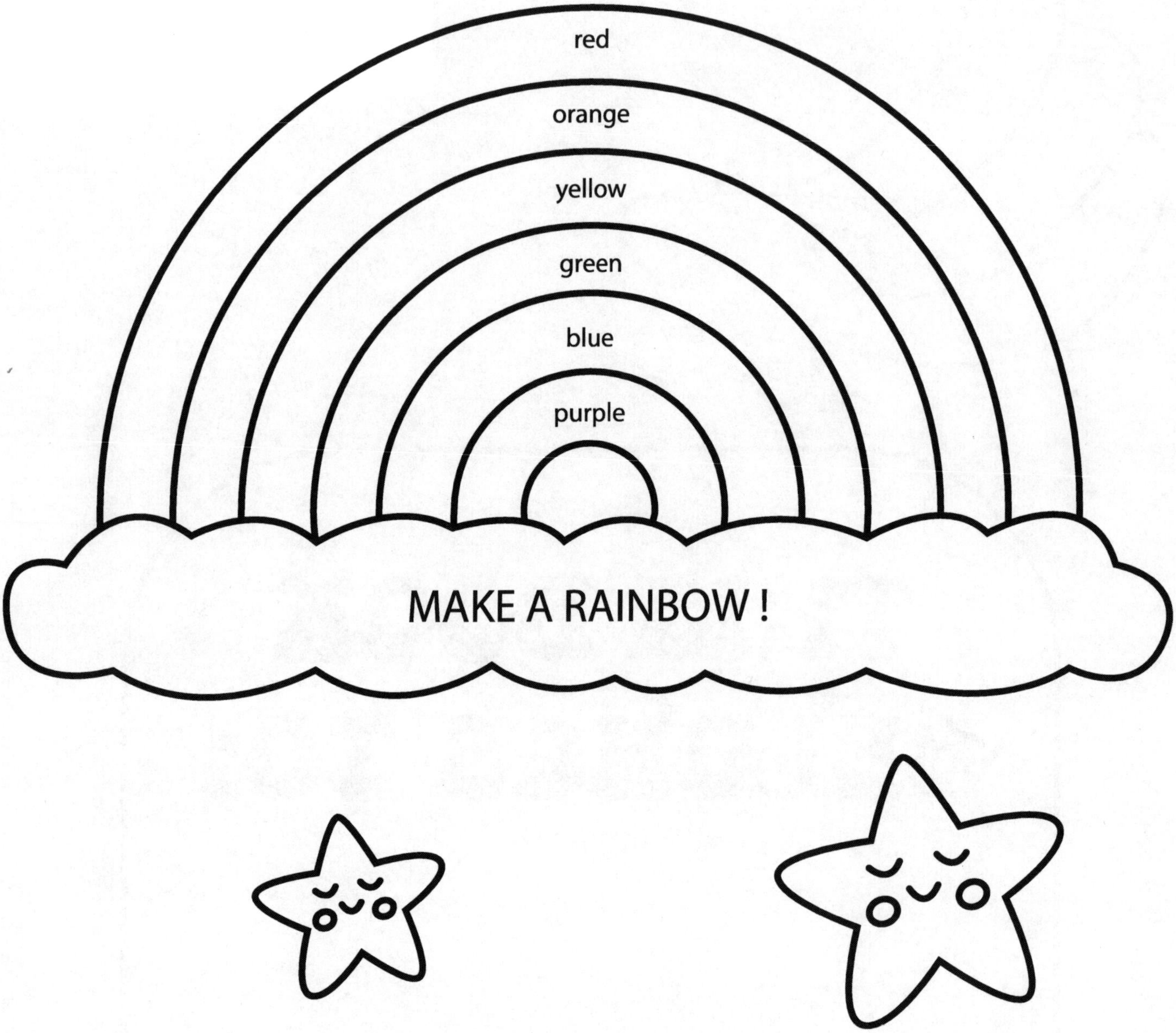
red
orange
yellow
green
blue
purple
MAKE A RAINBOW !

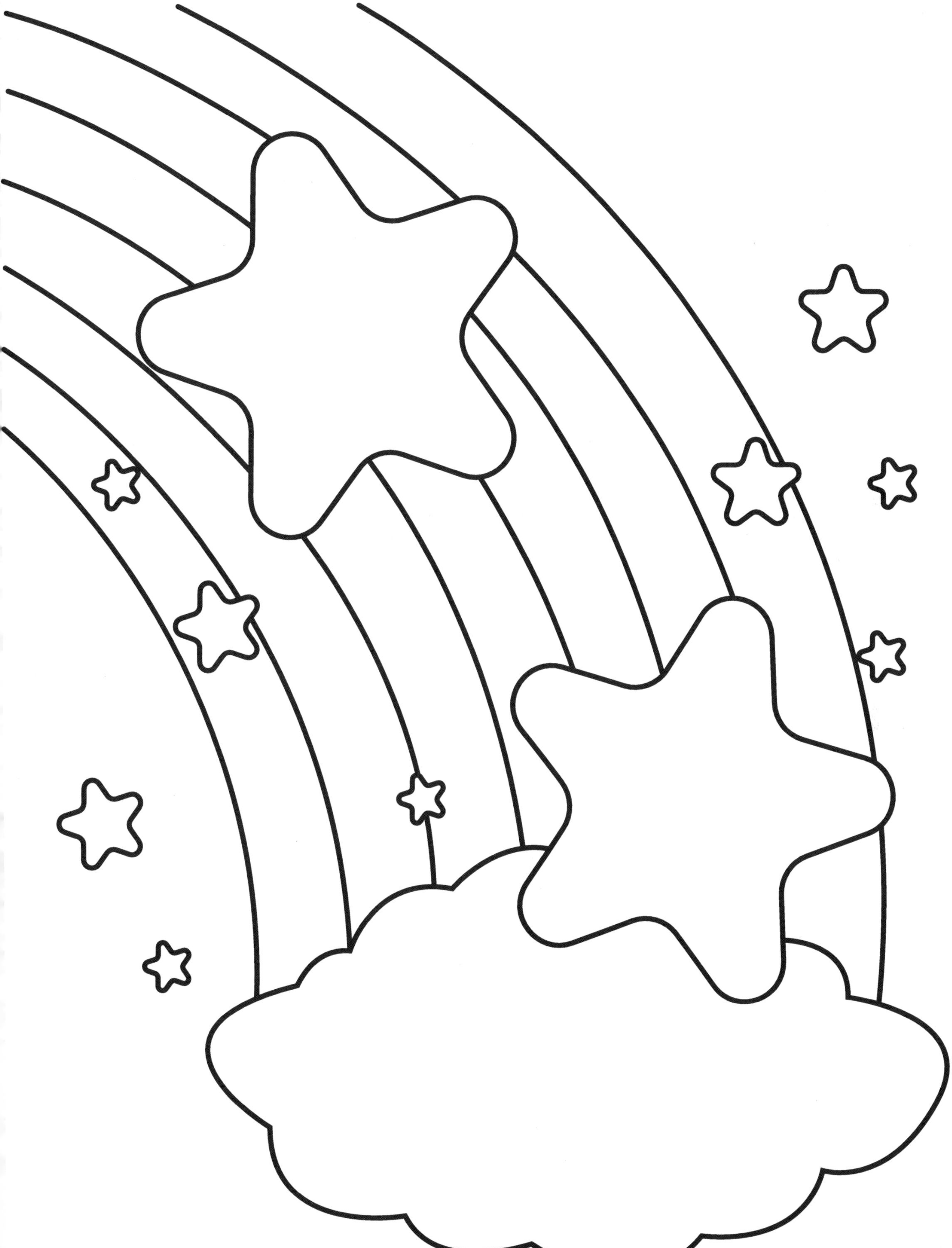

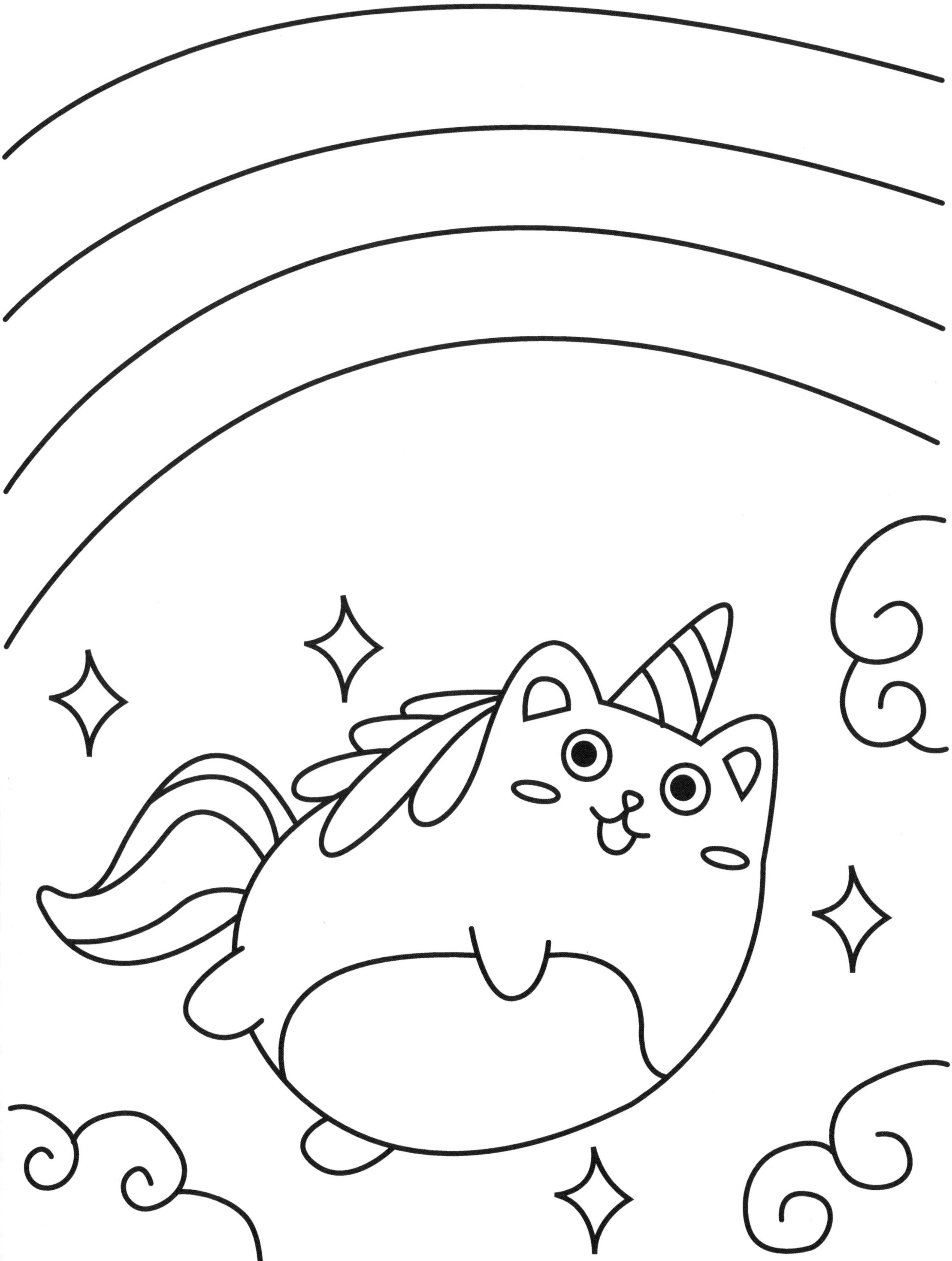

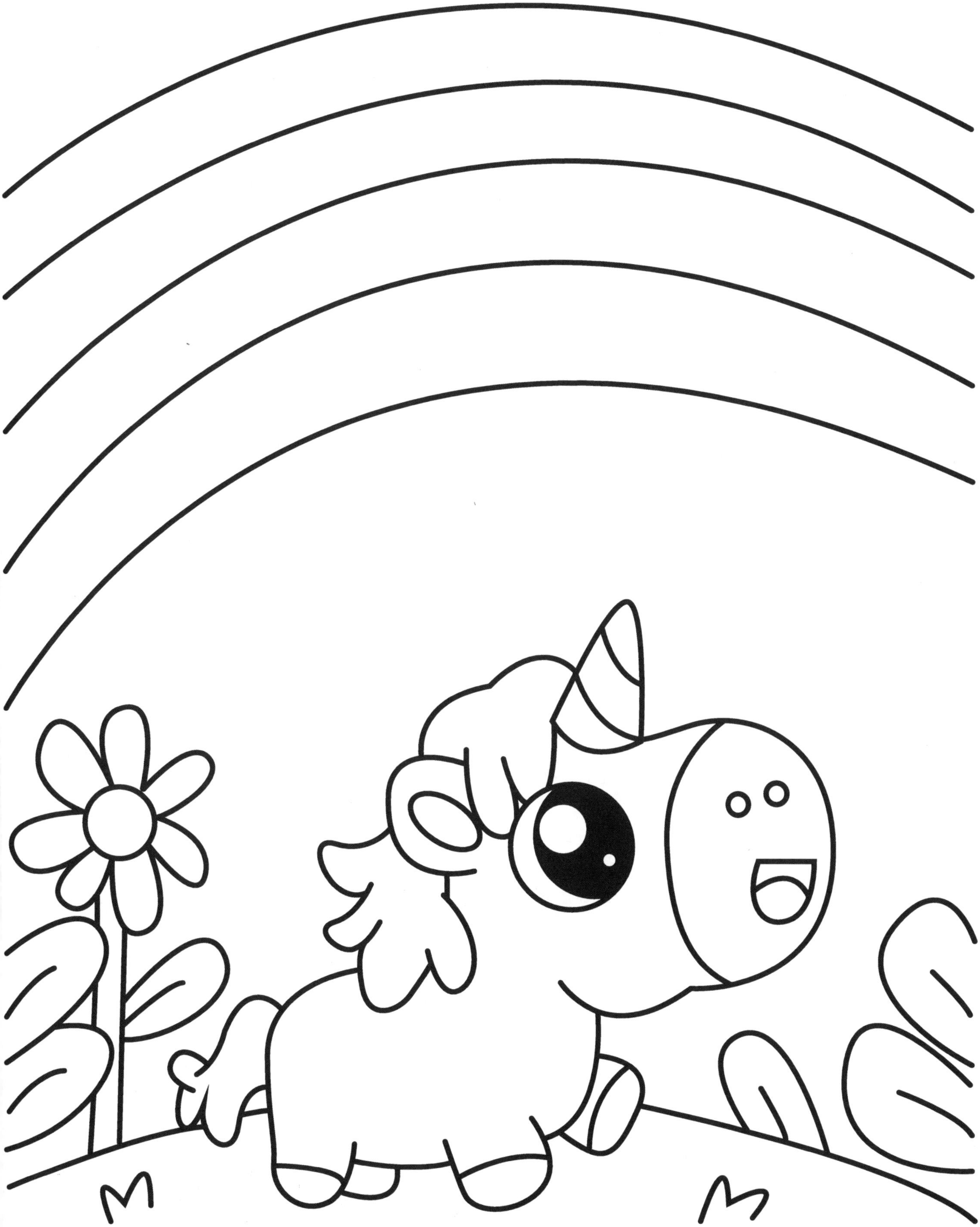

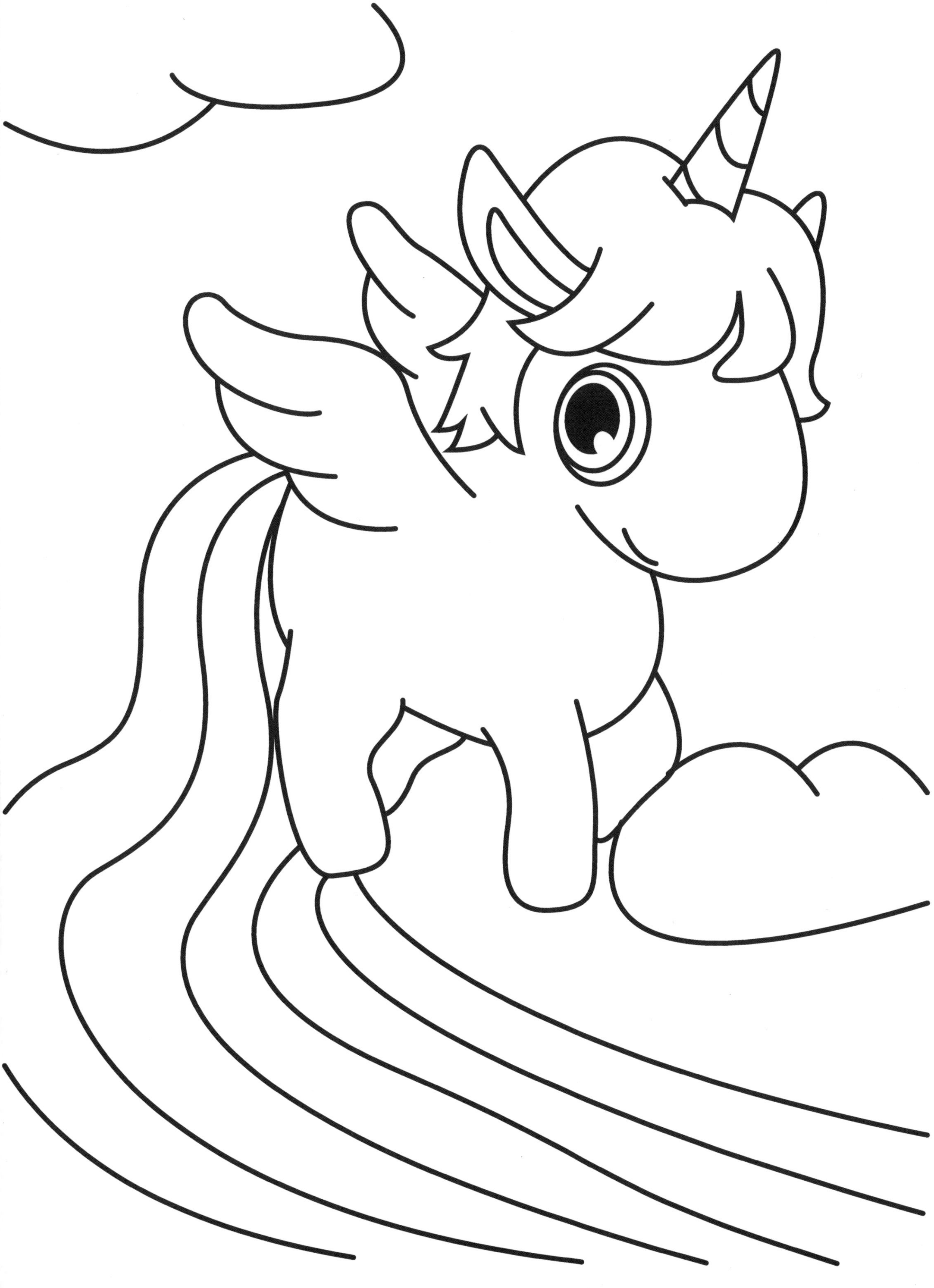

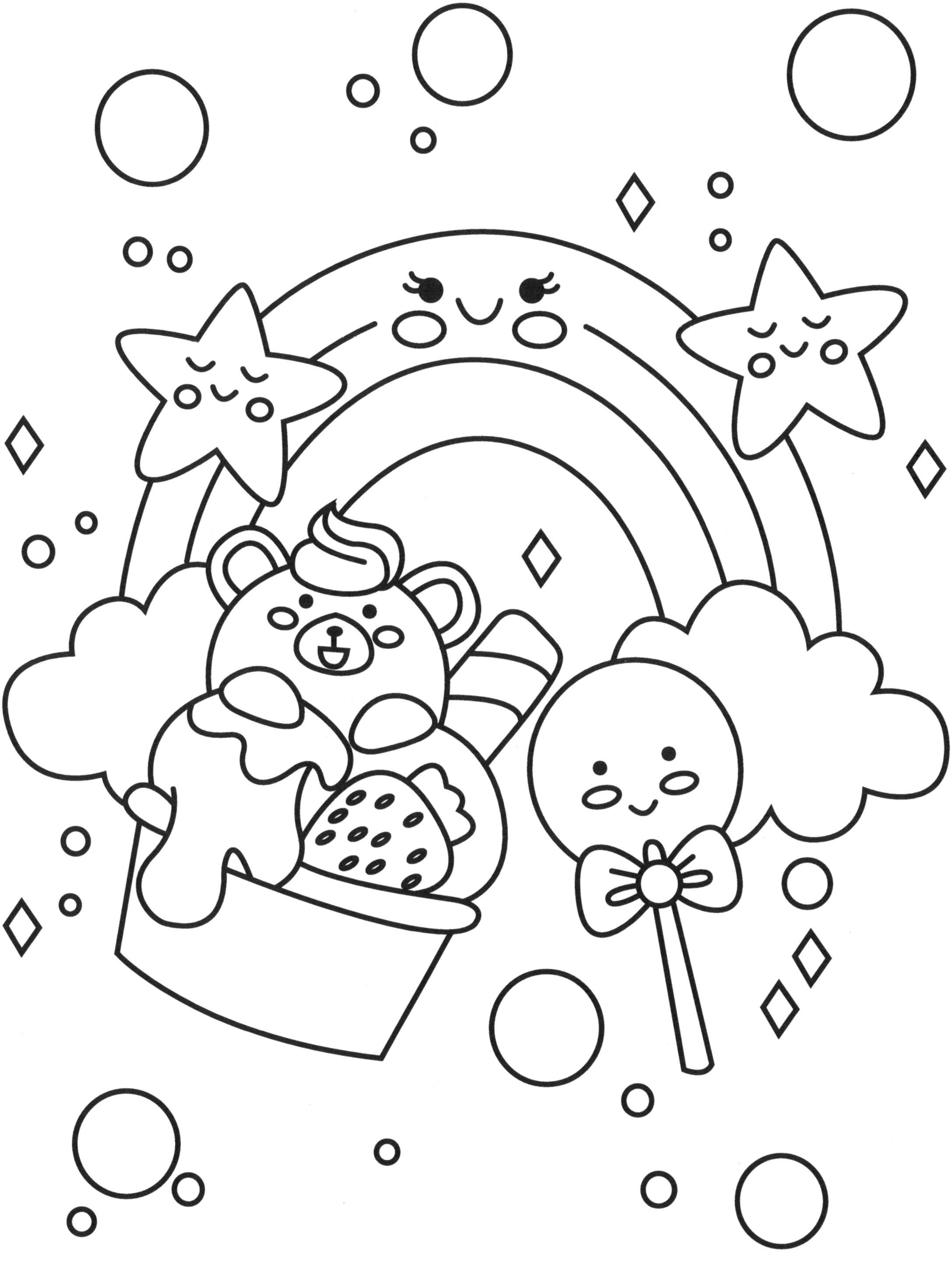

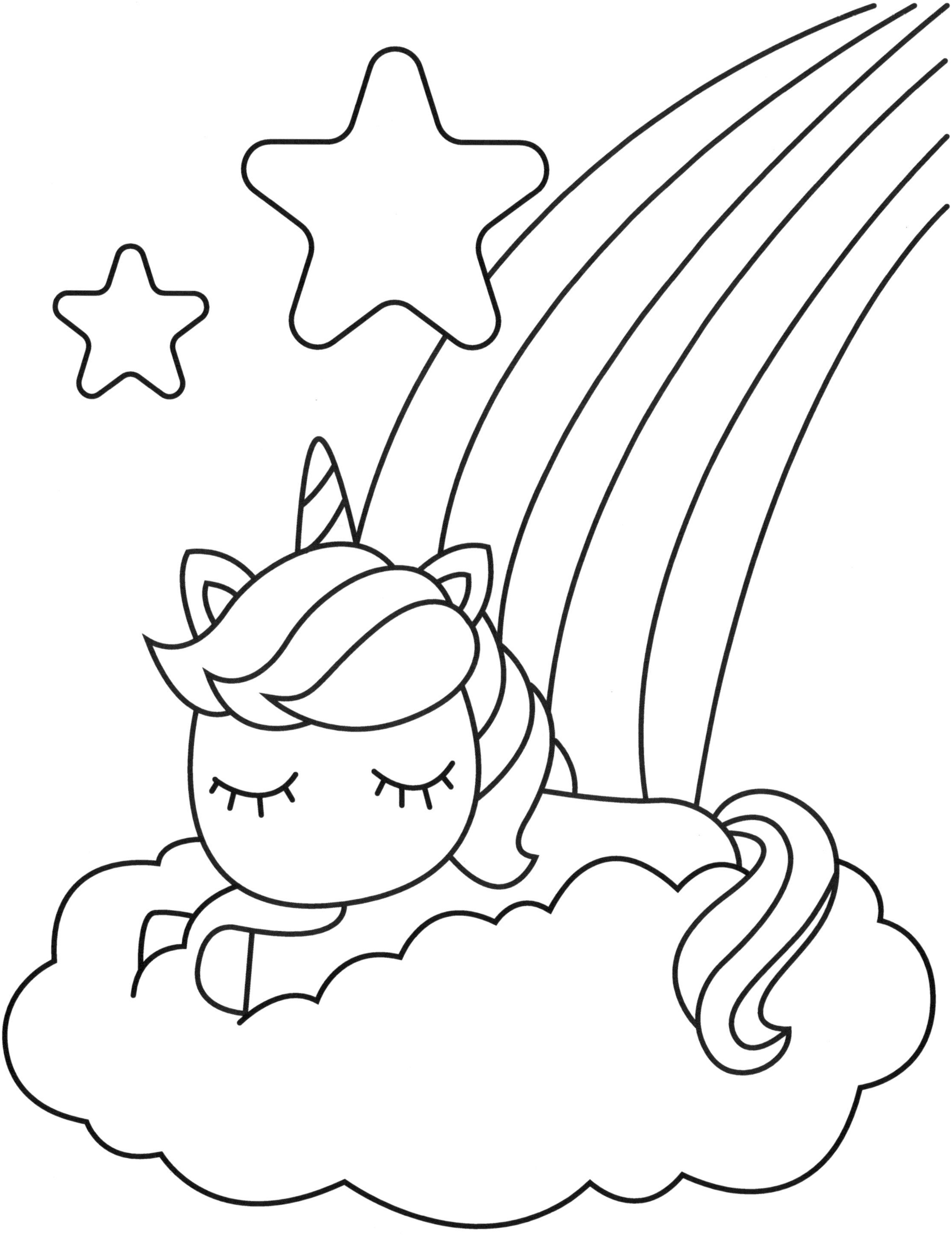

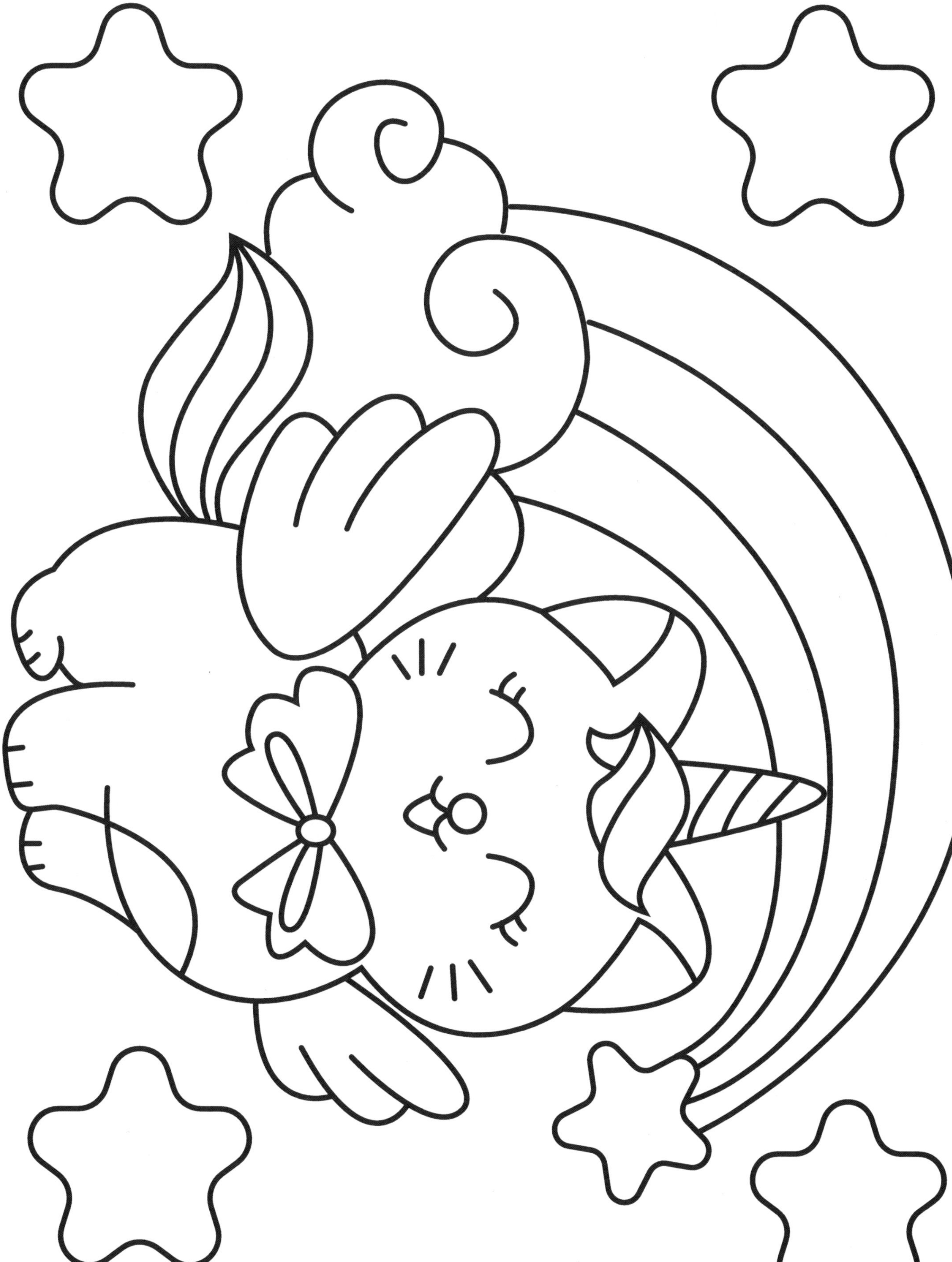

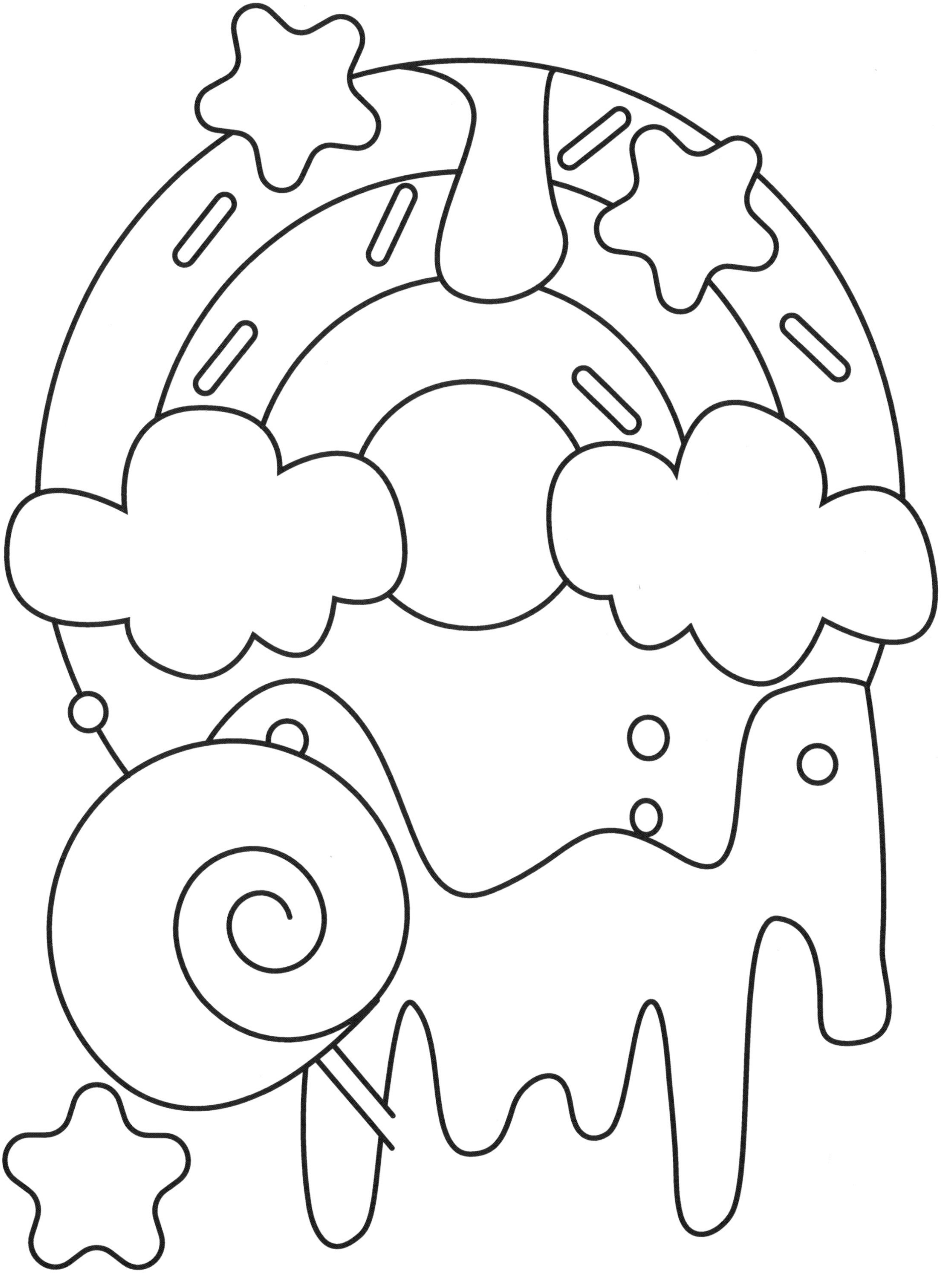

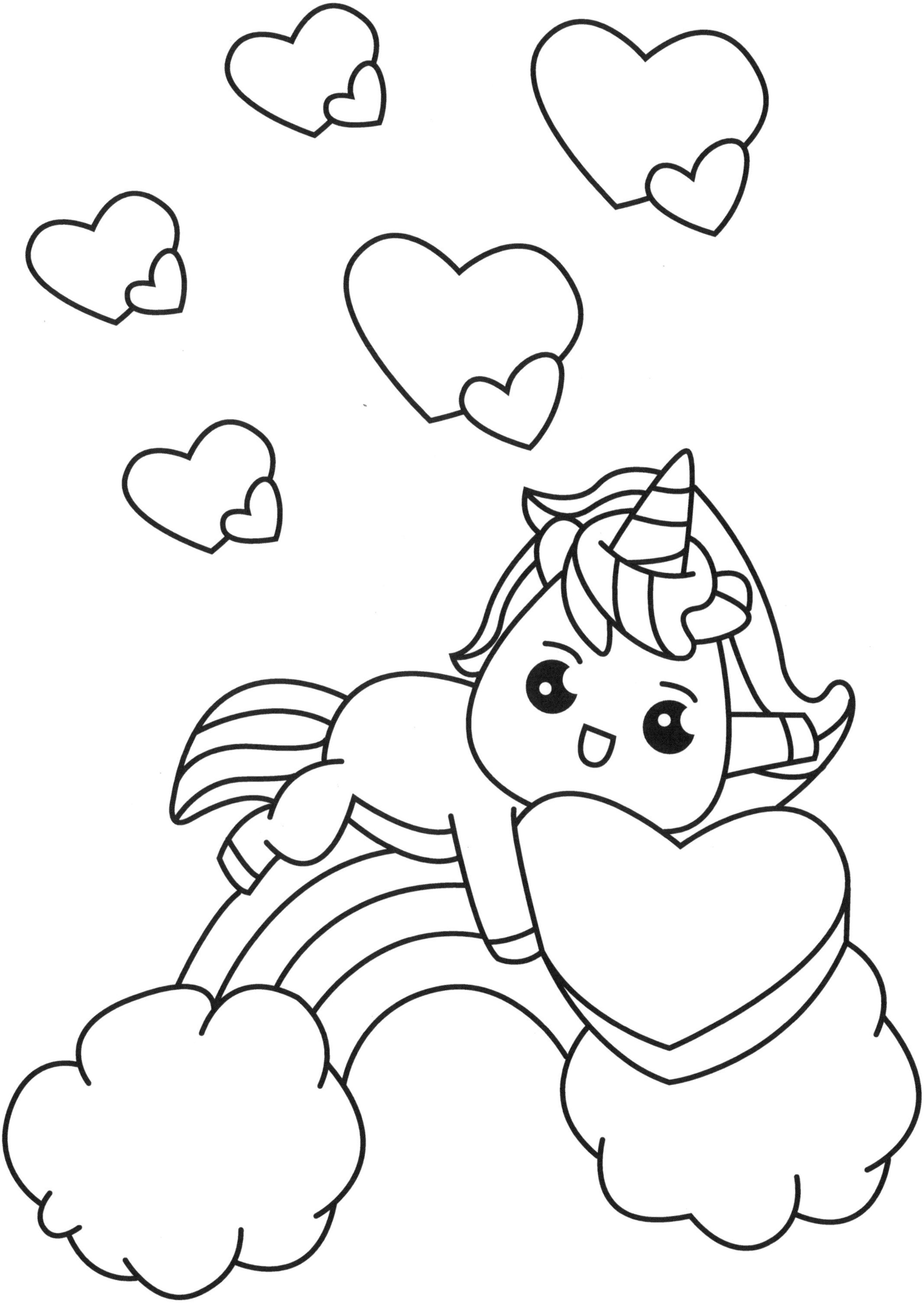

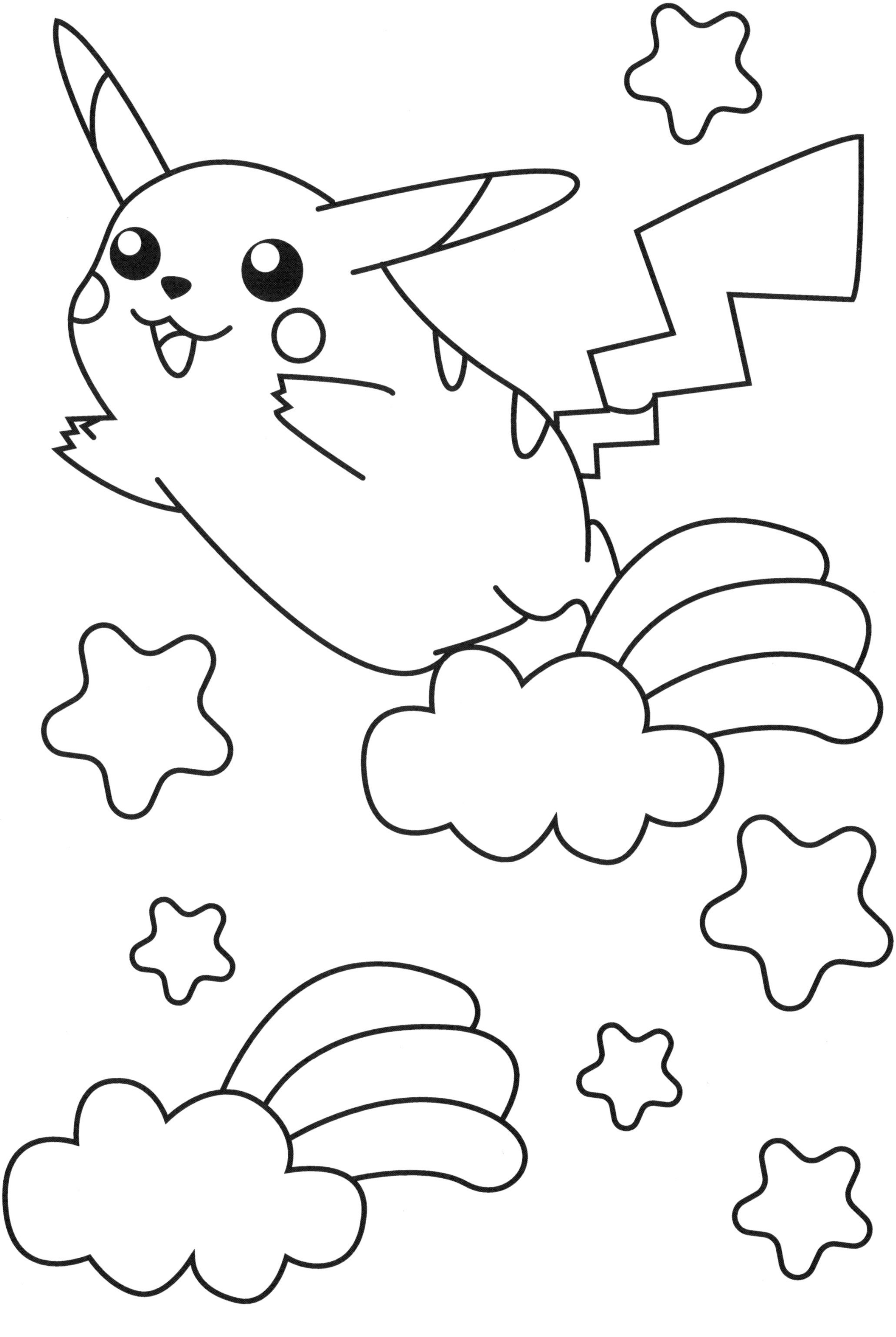

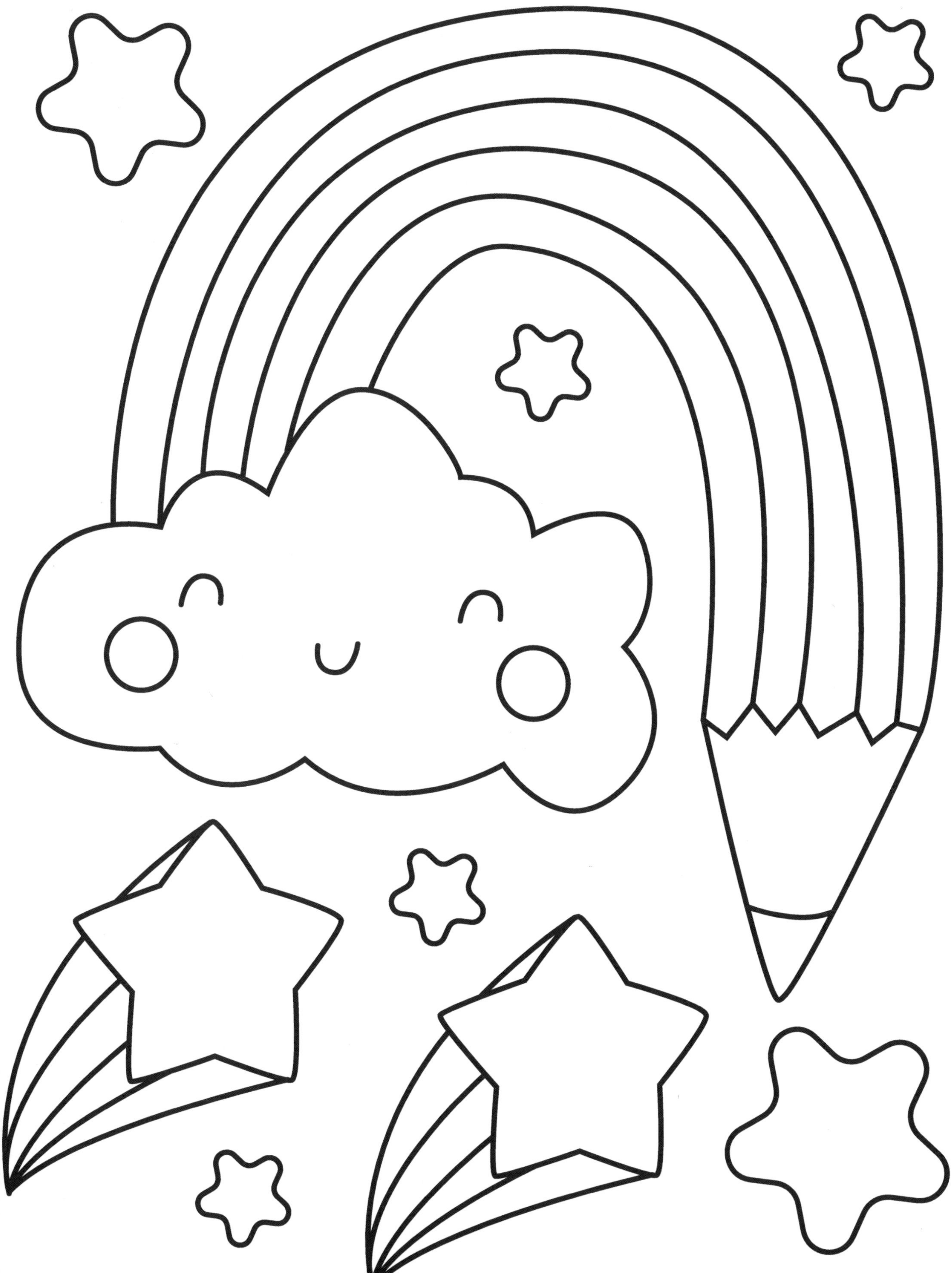

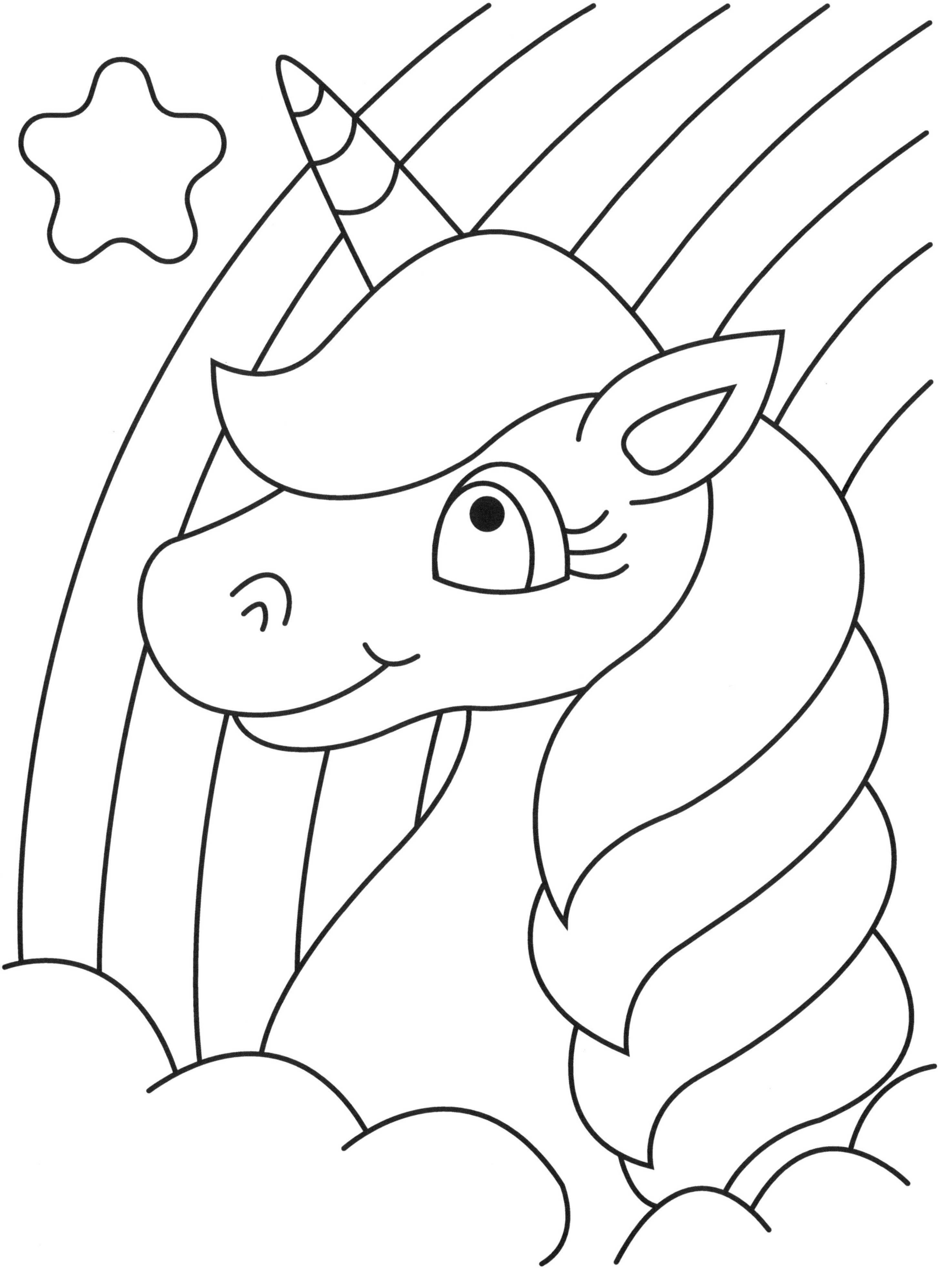

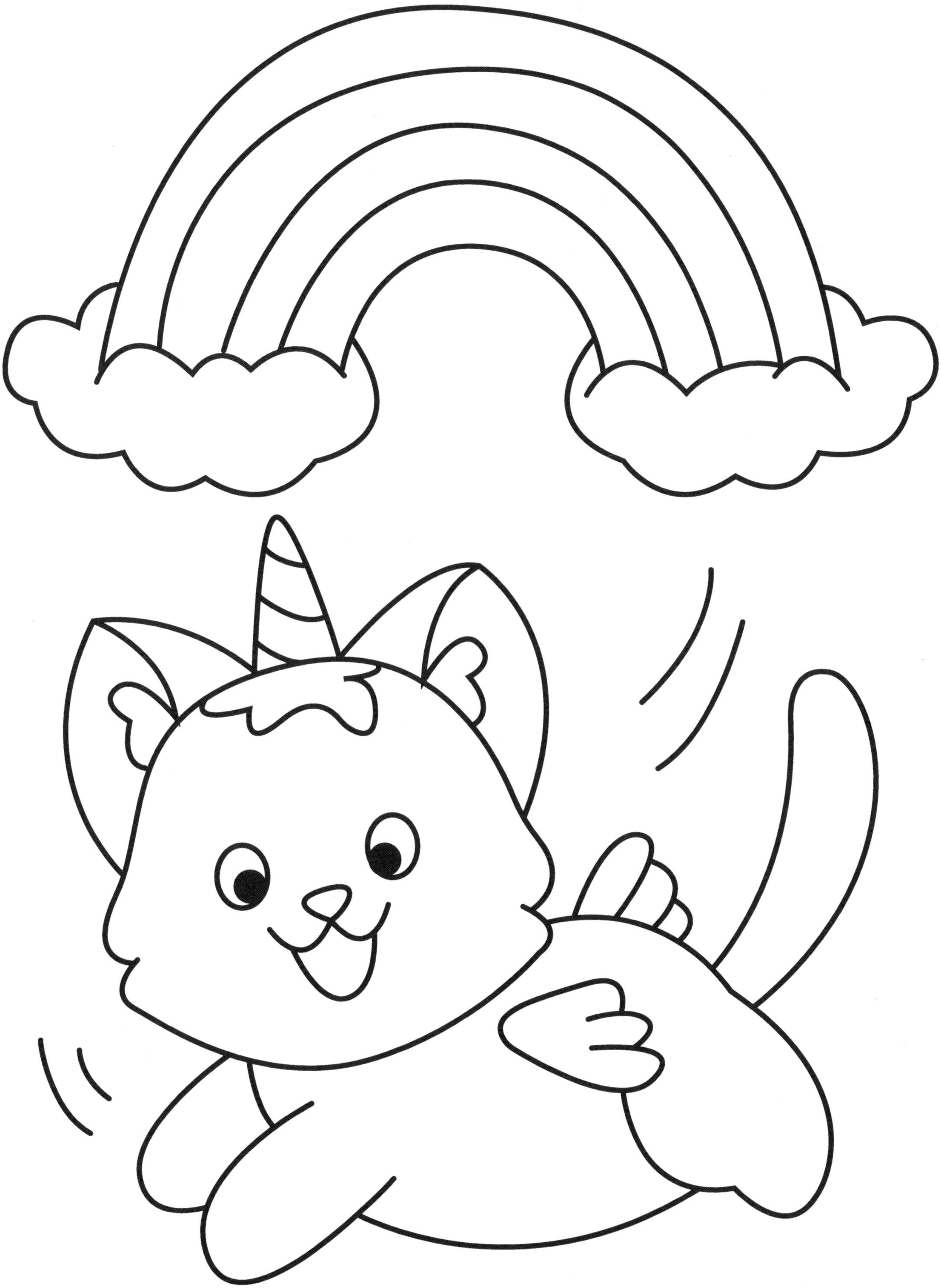

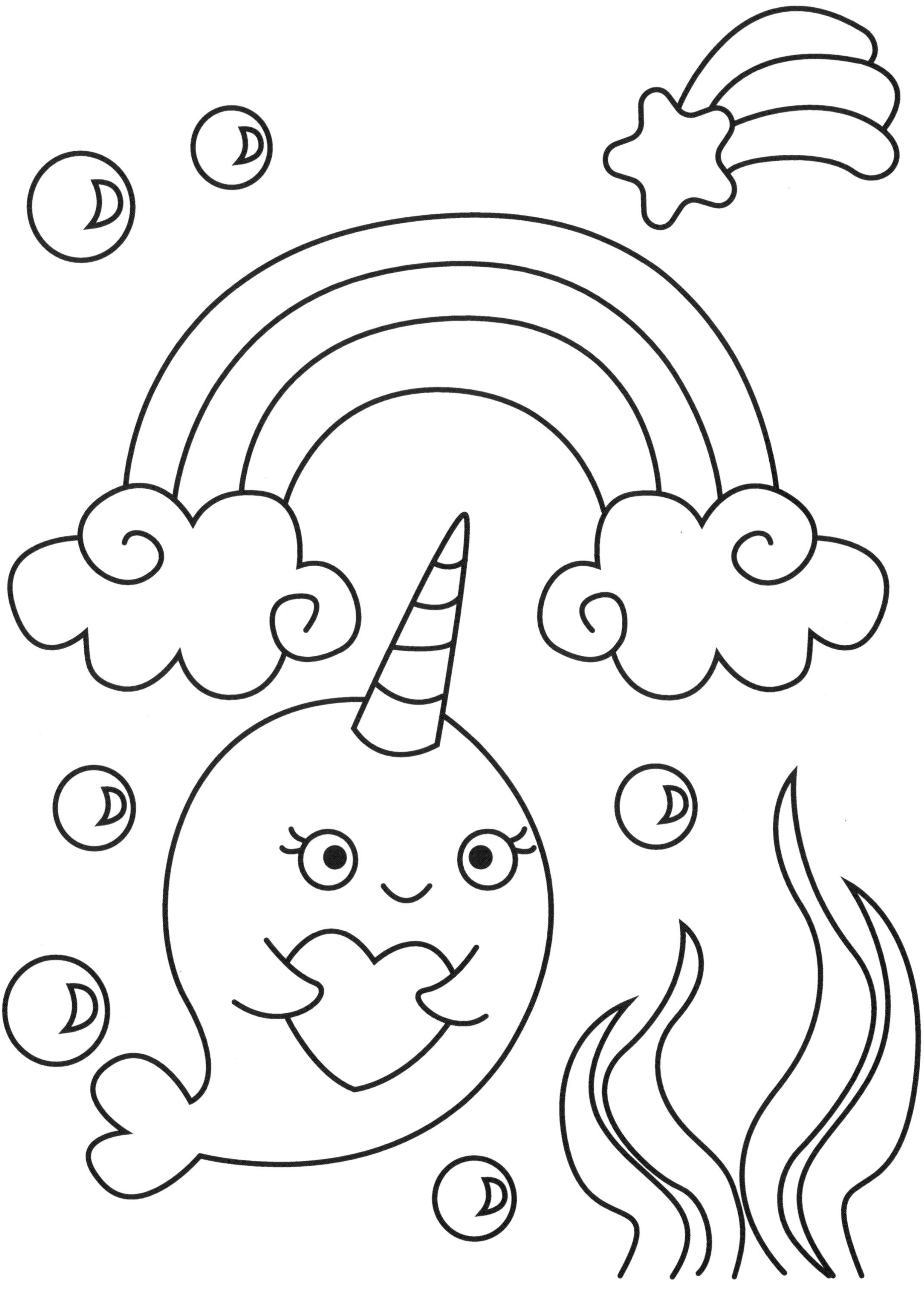

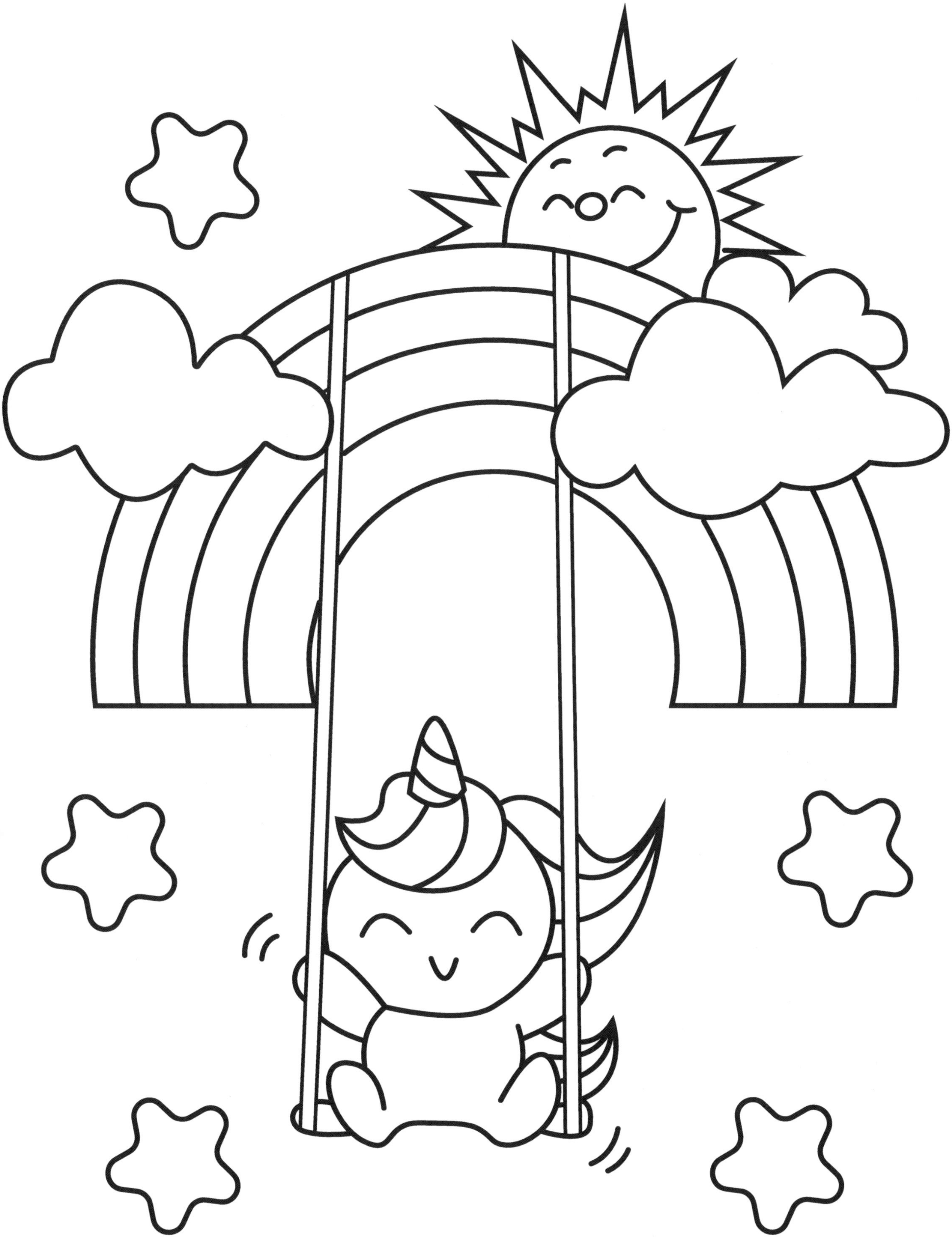

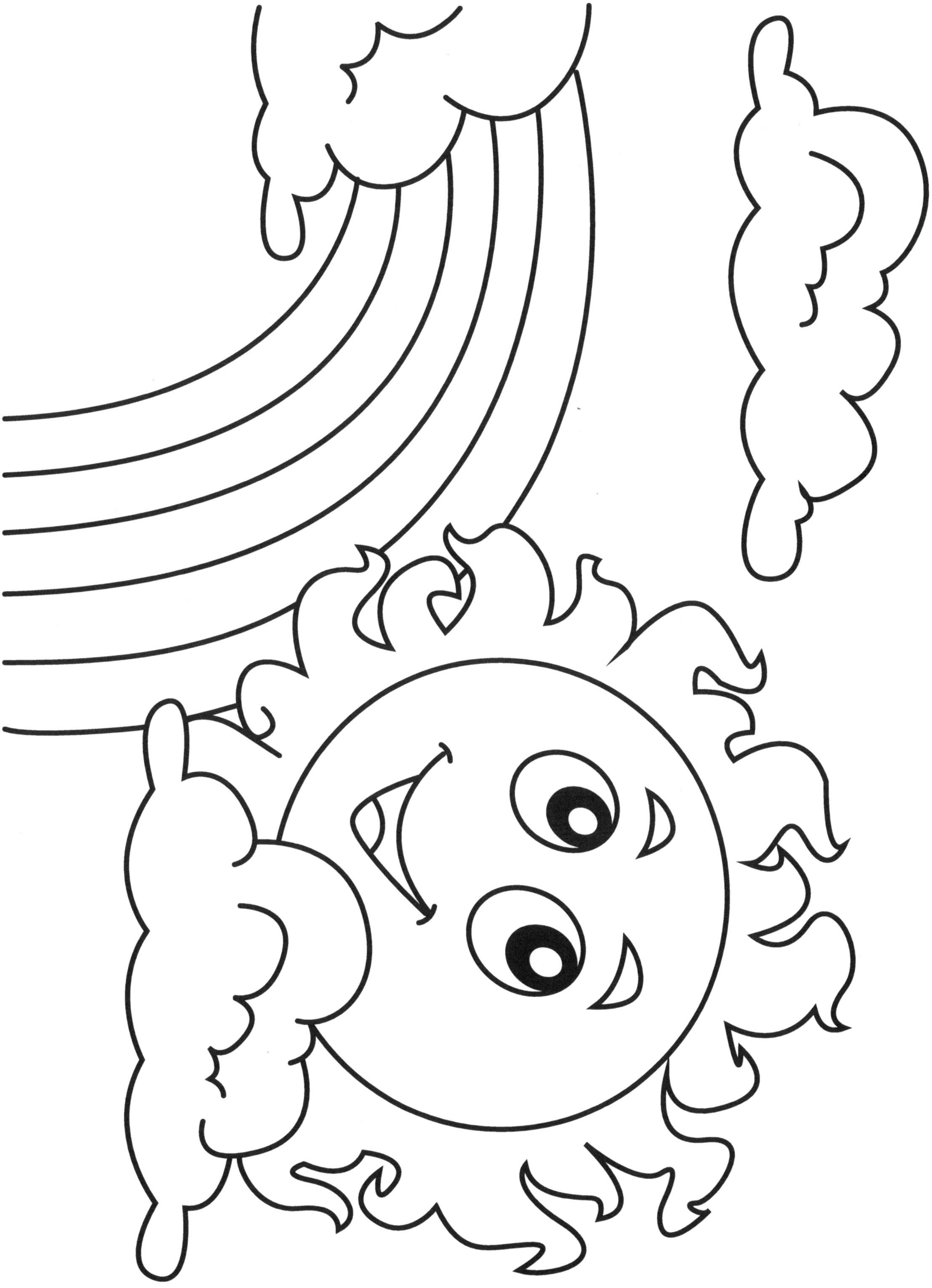

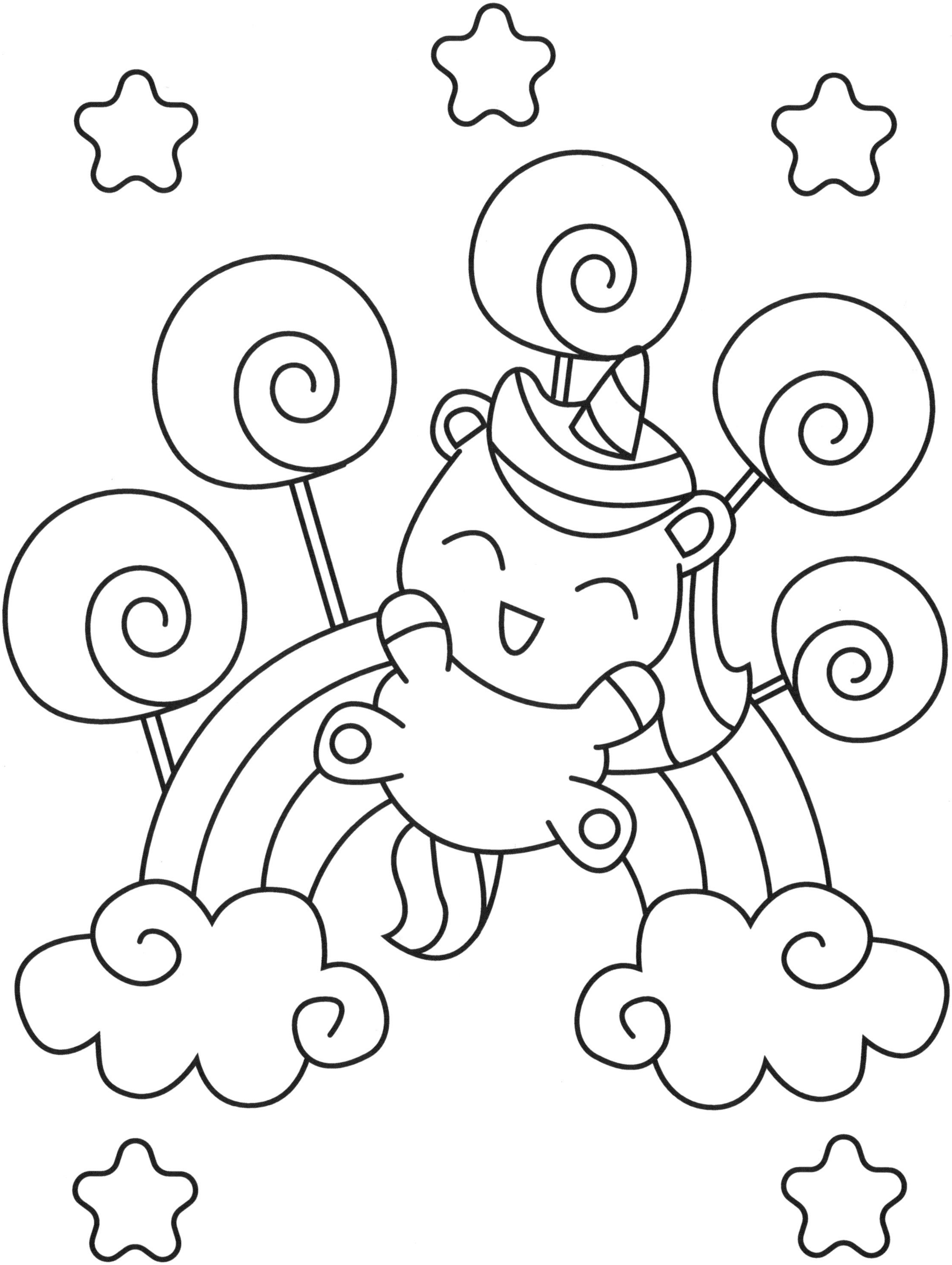

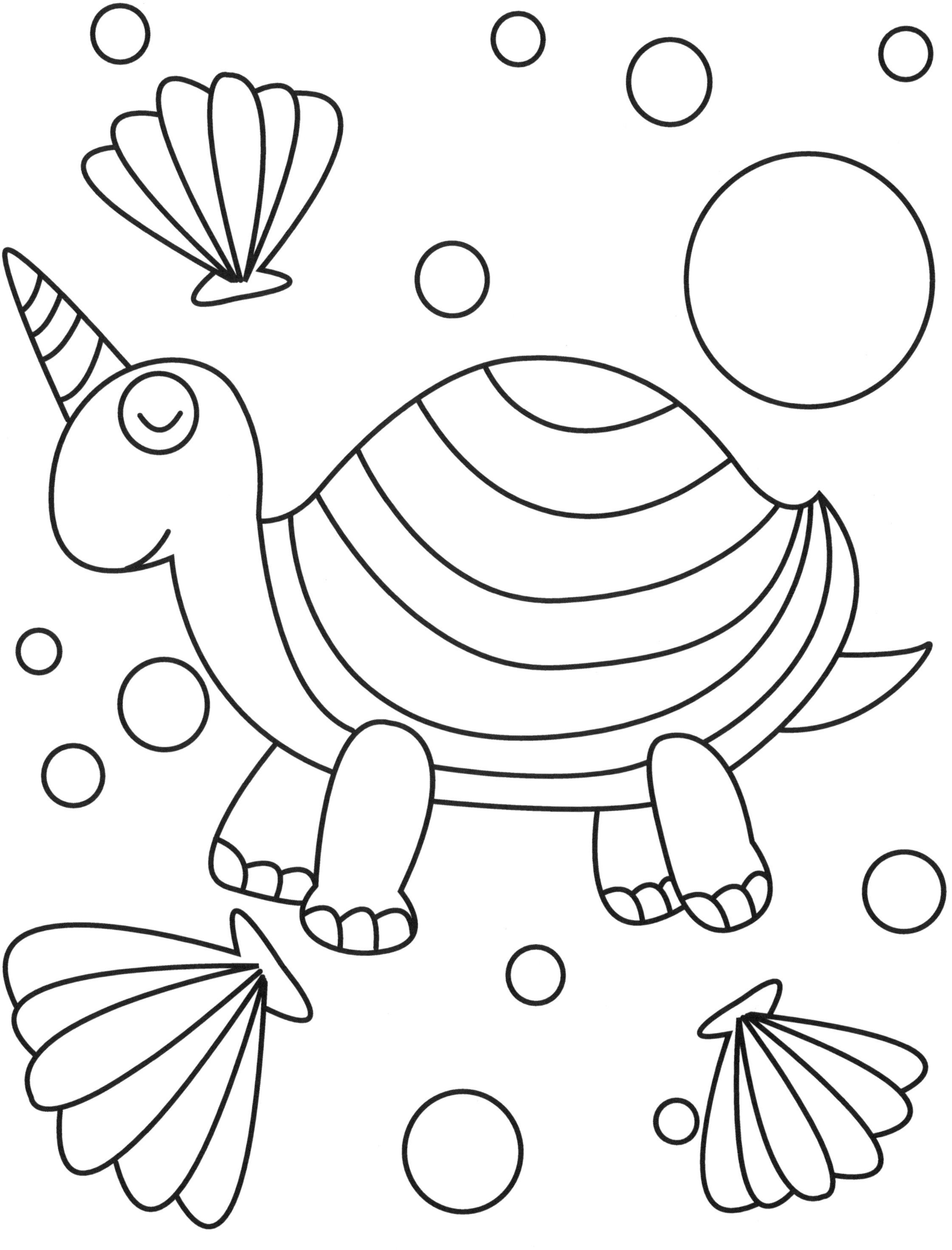

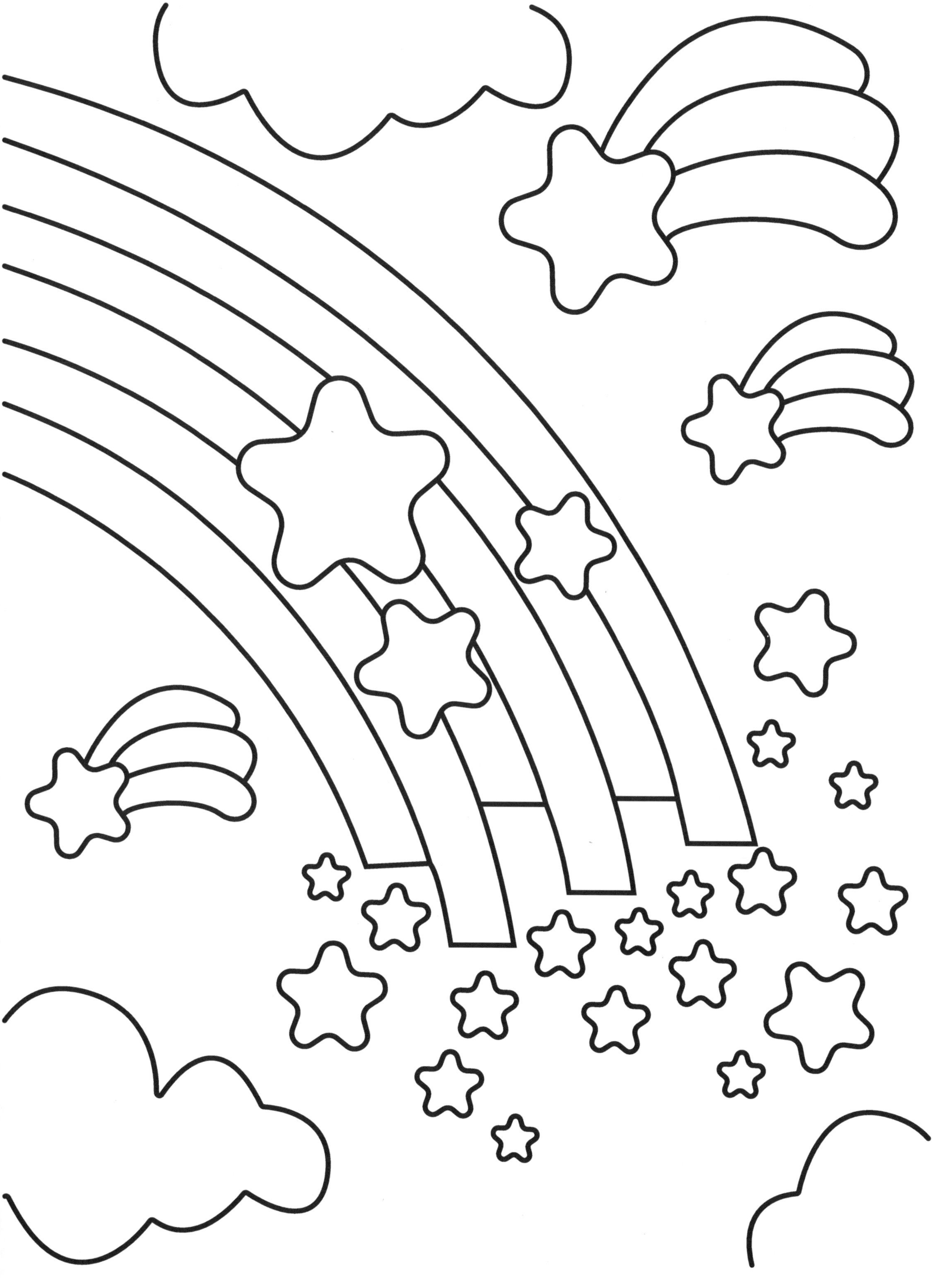

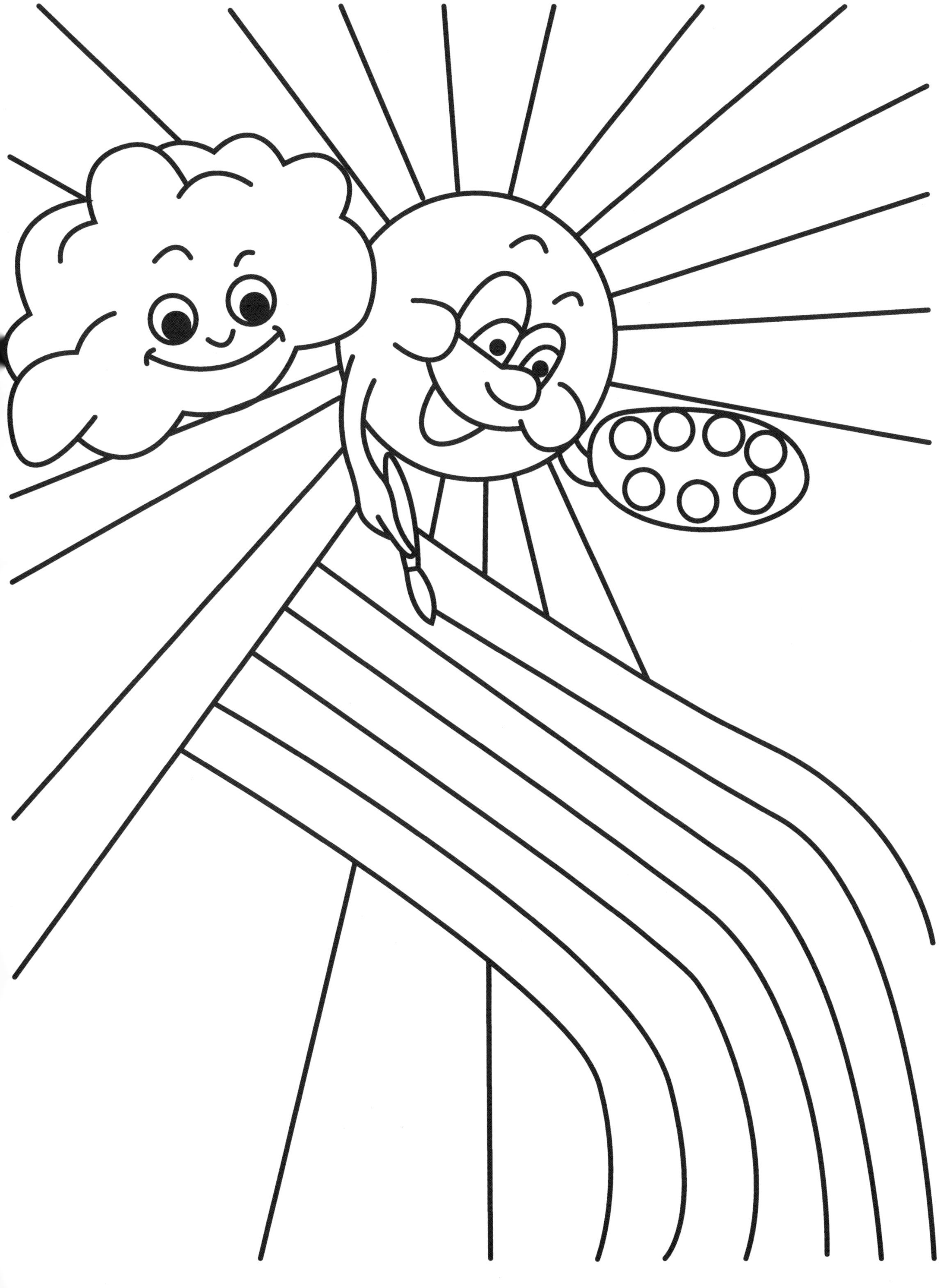

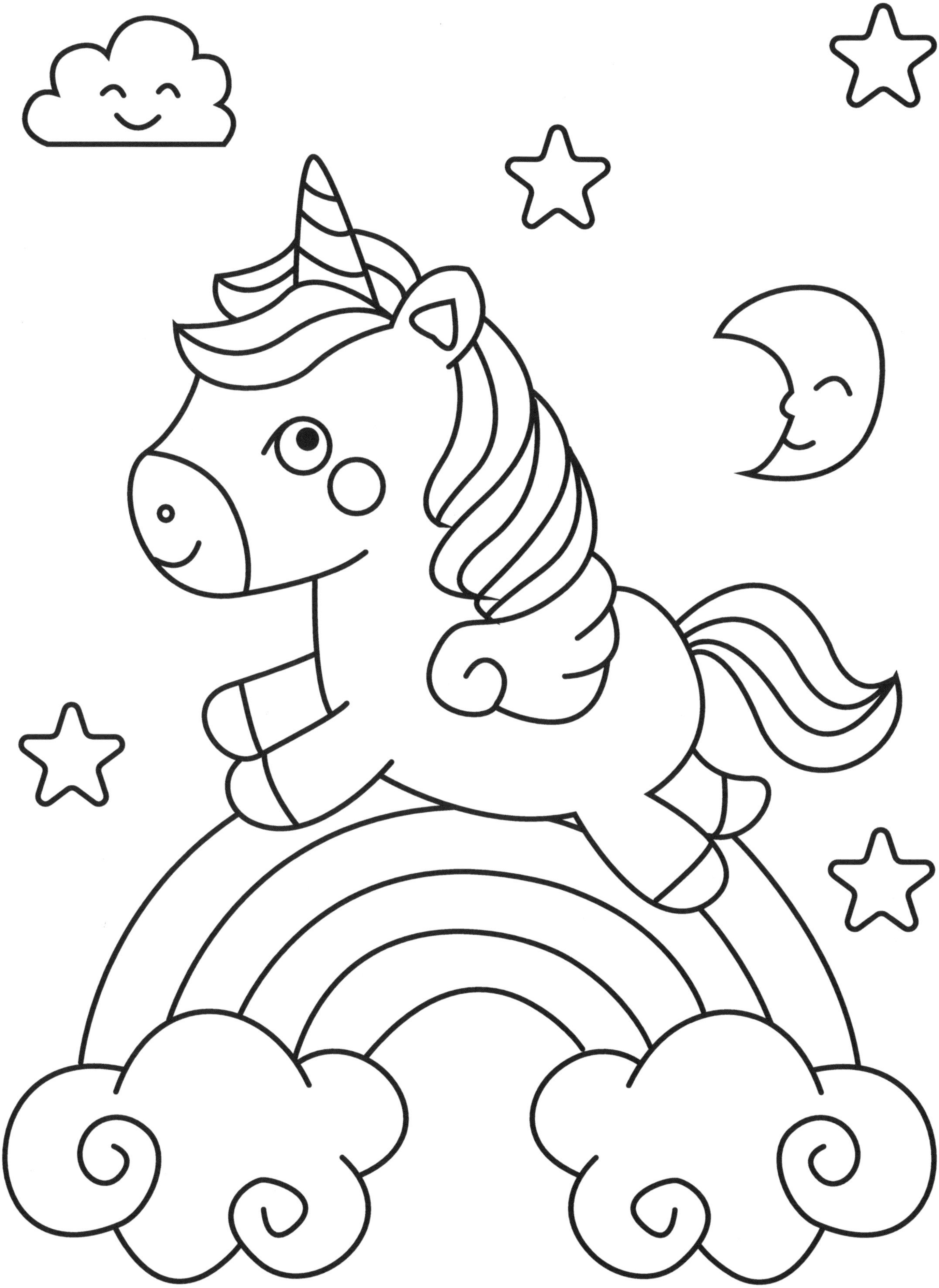

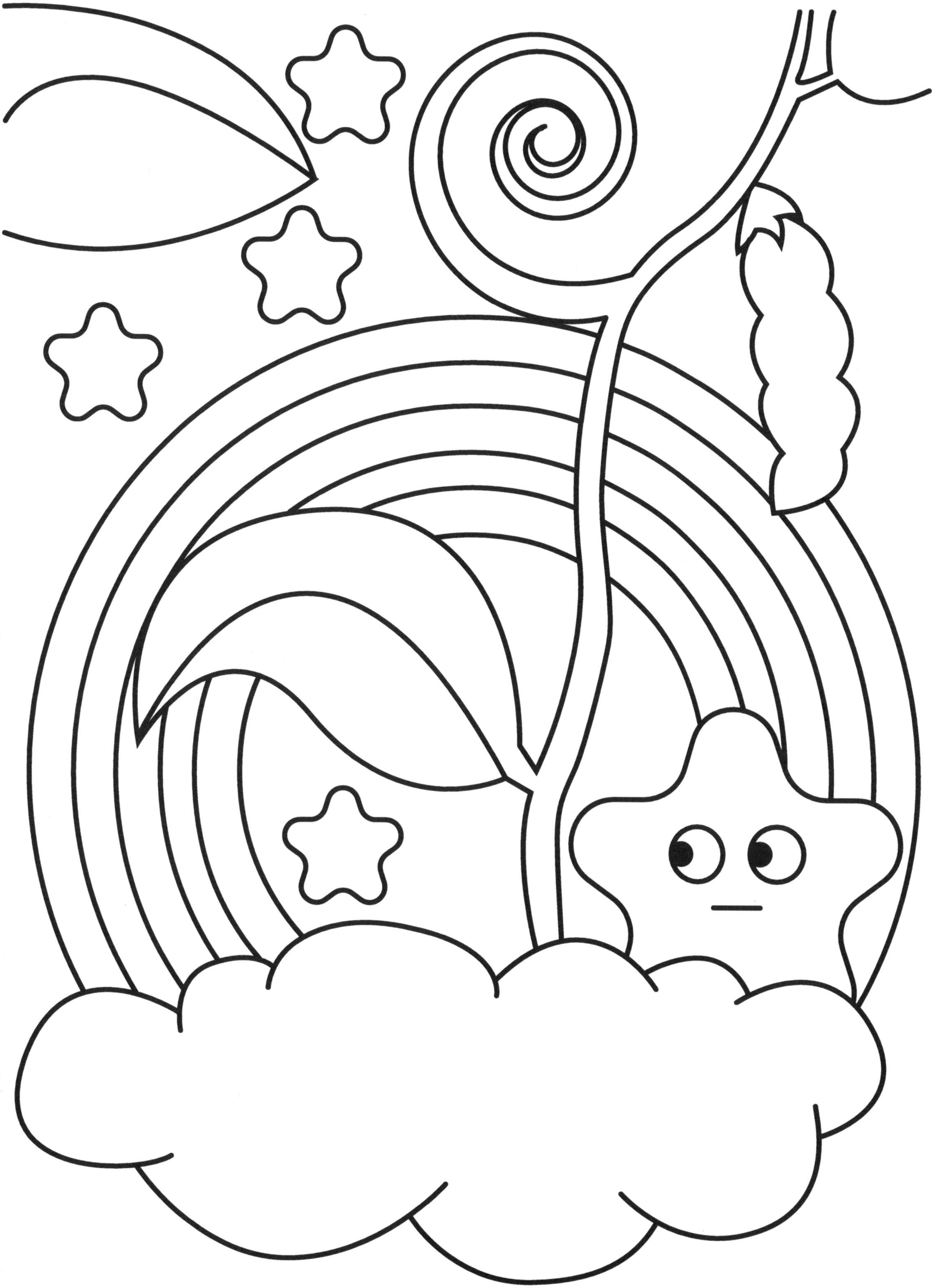

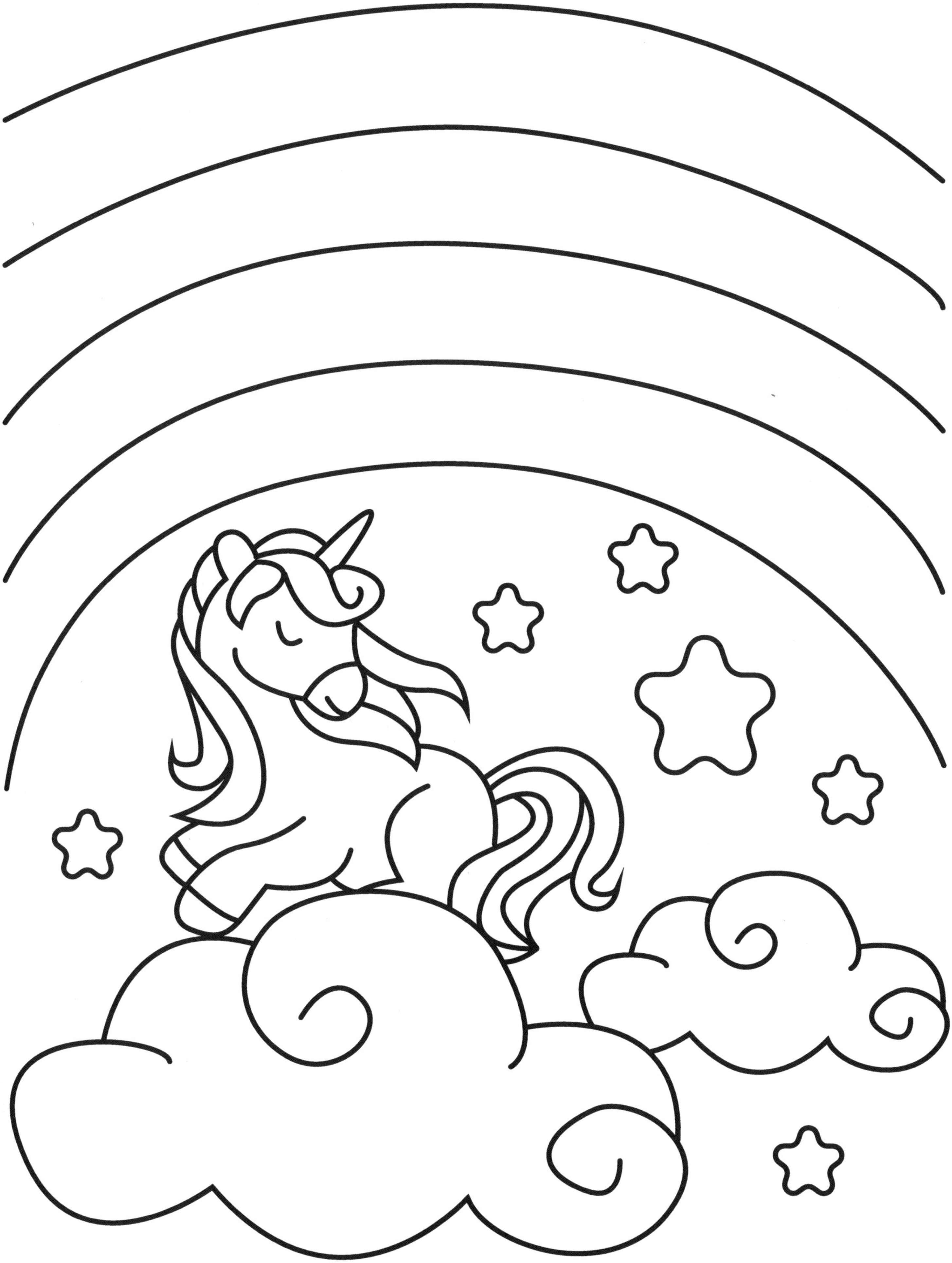

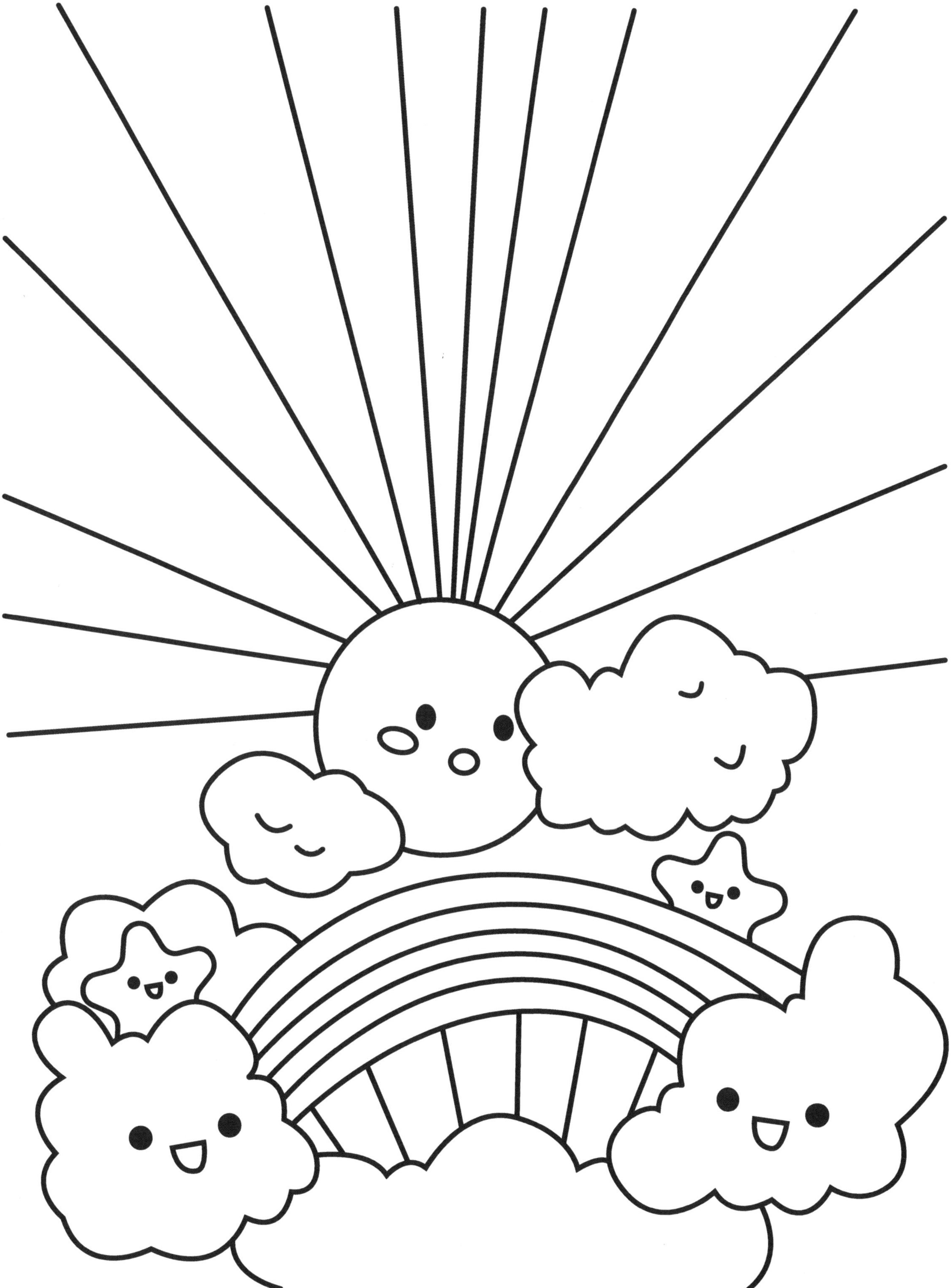

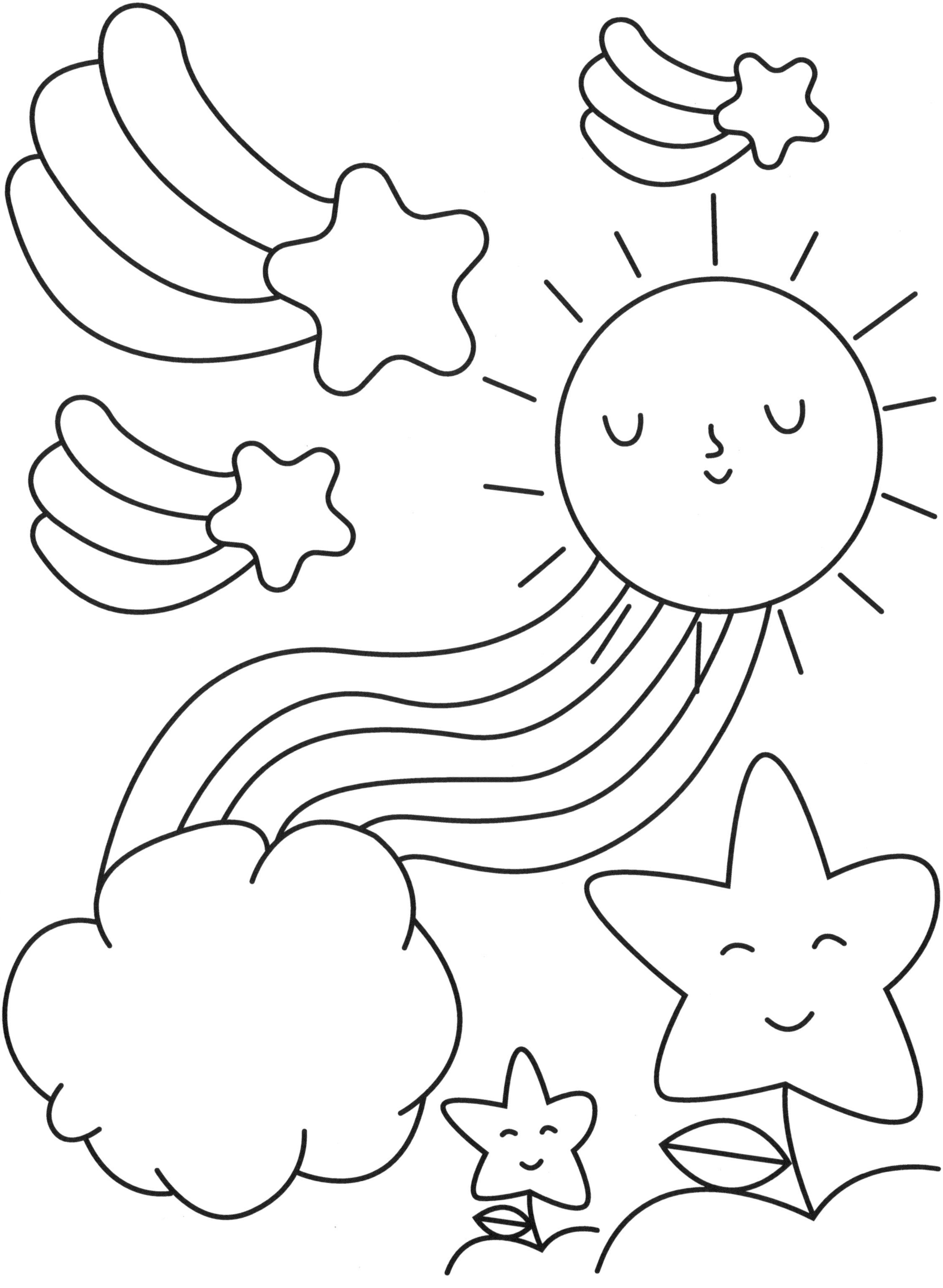

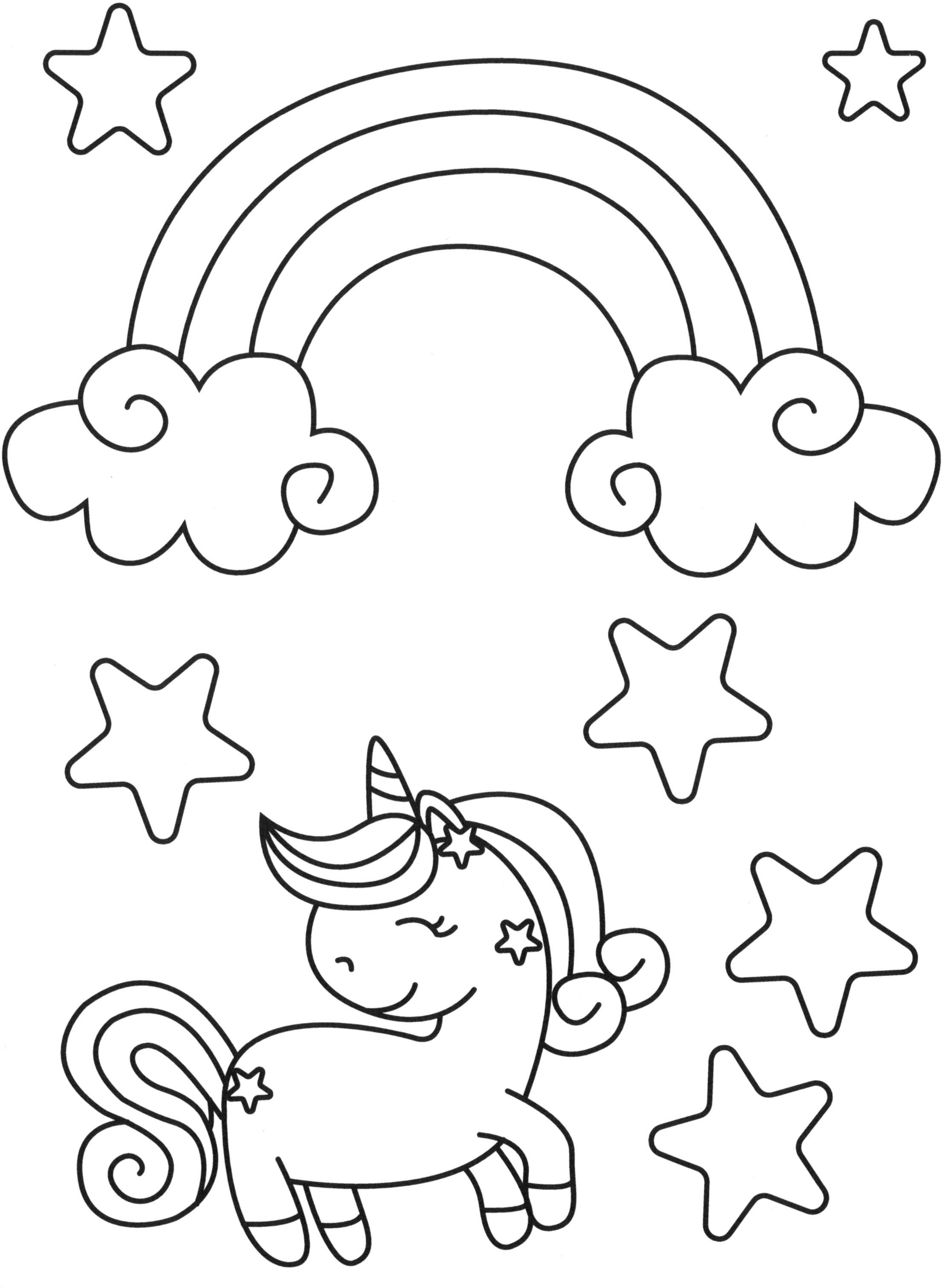

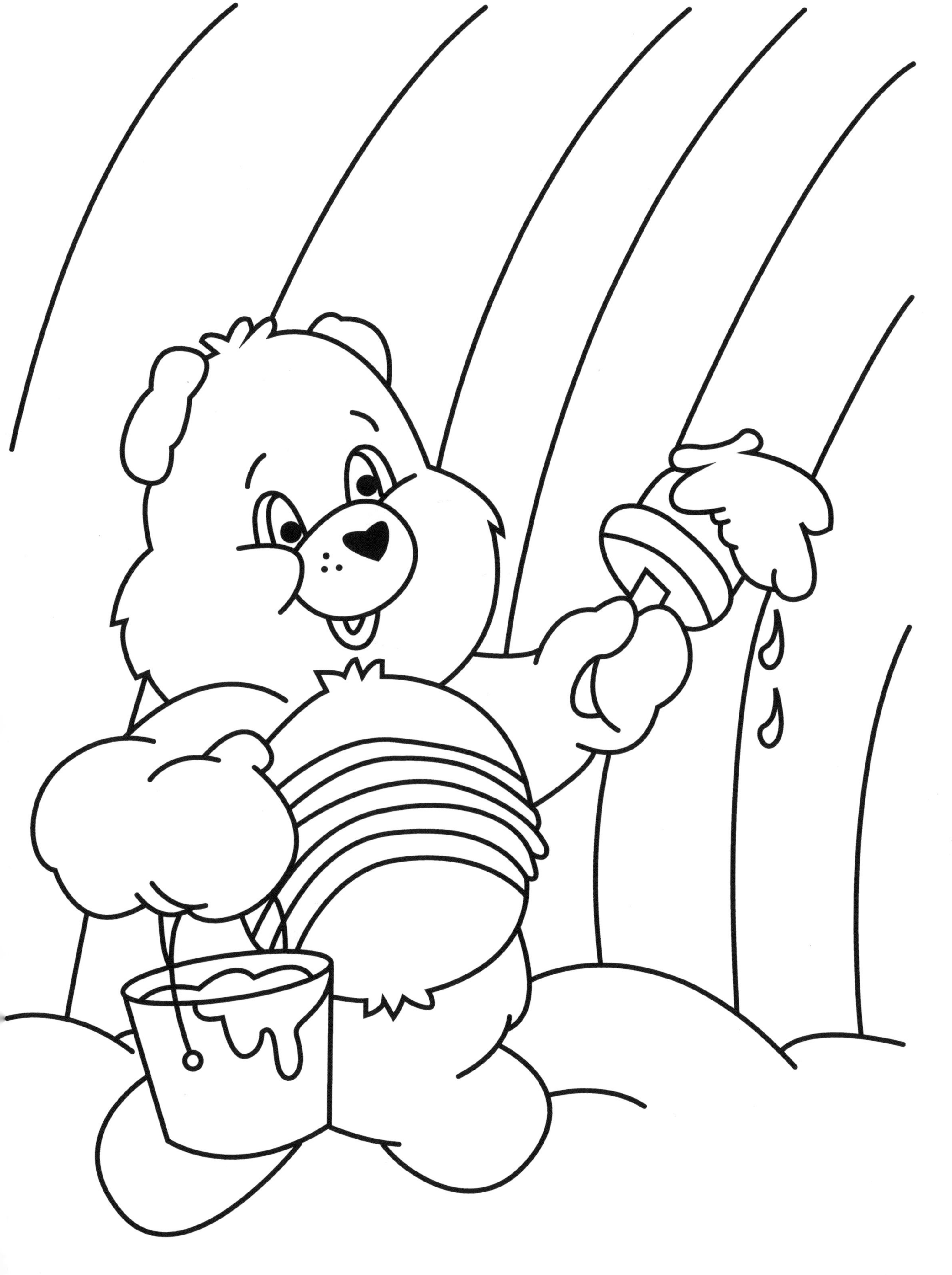

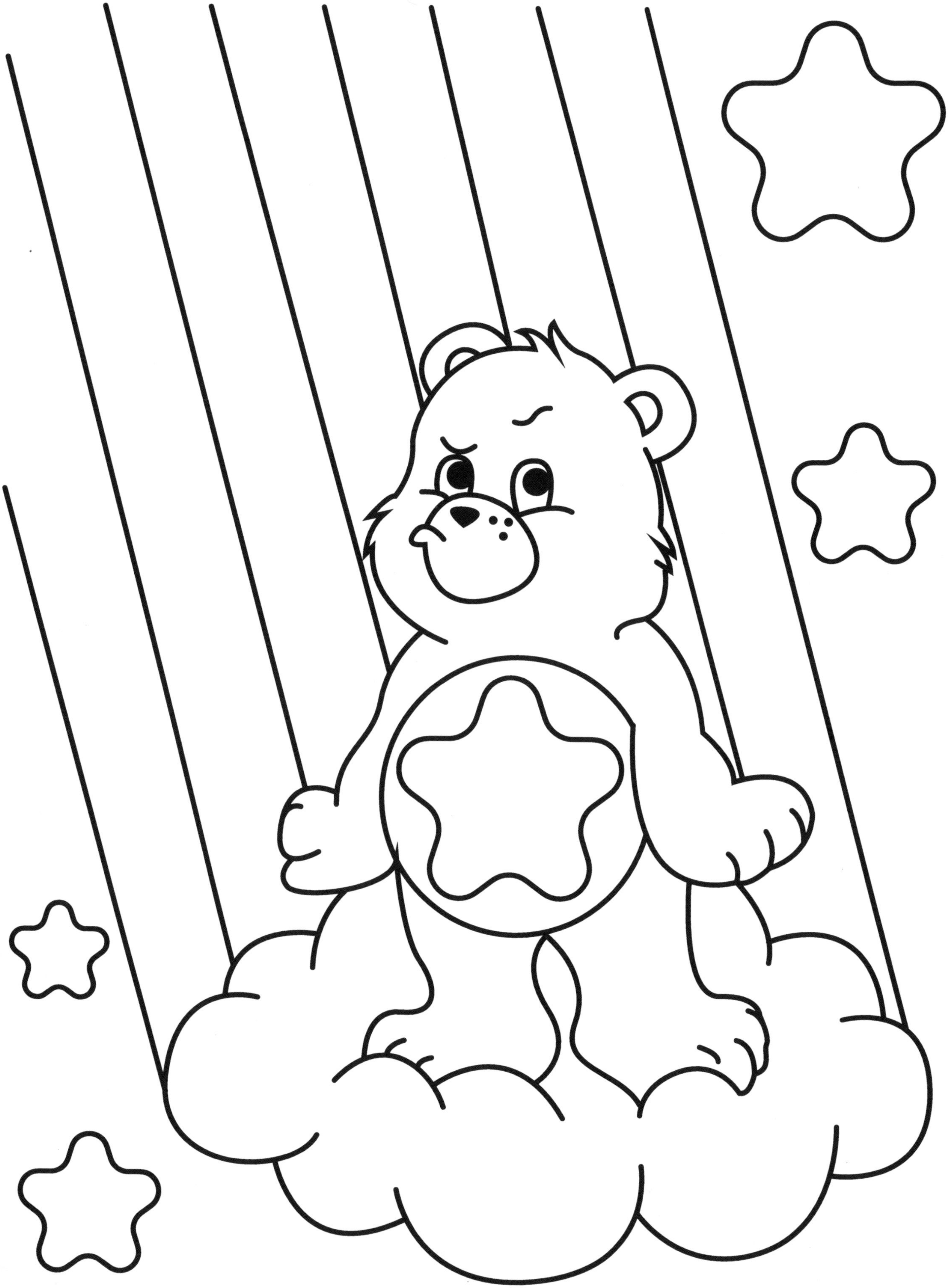

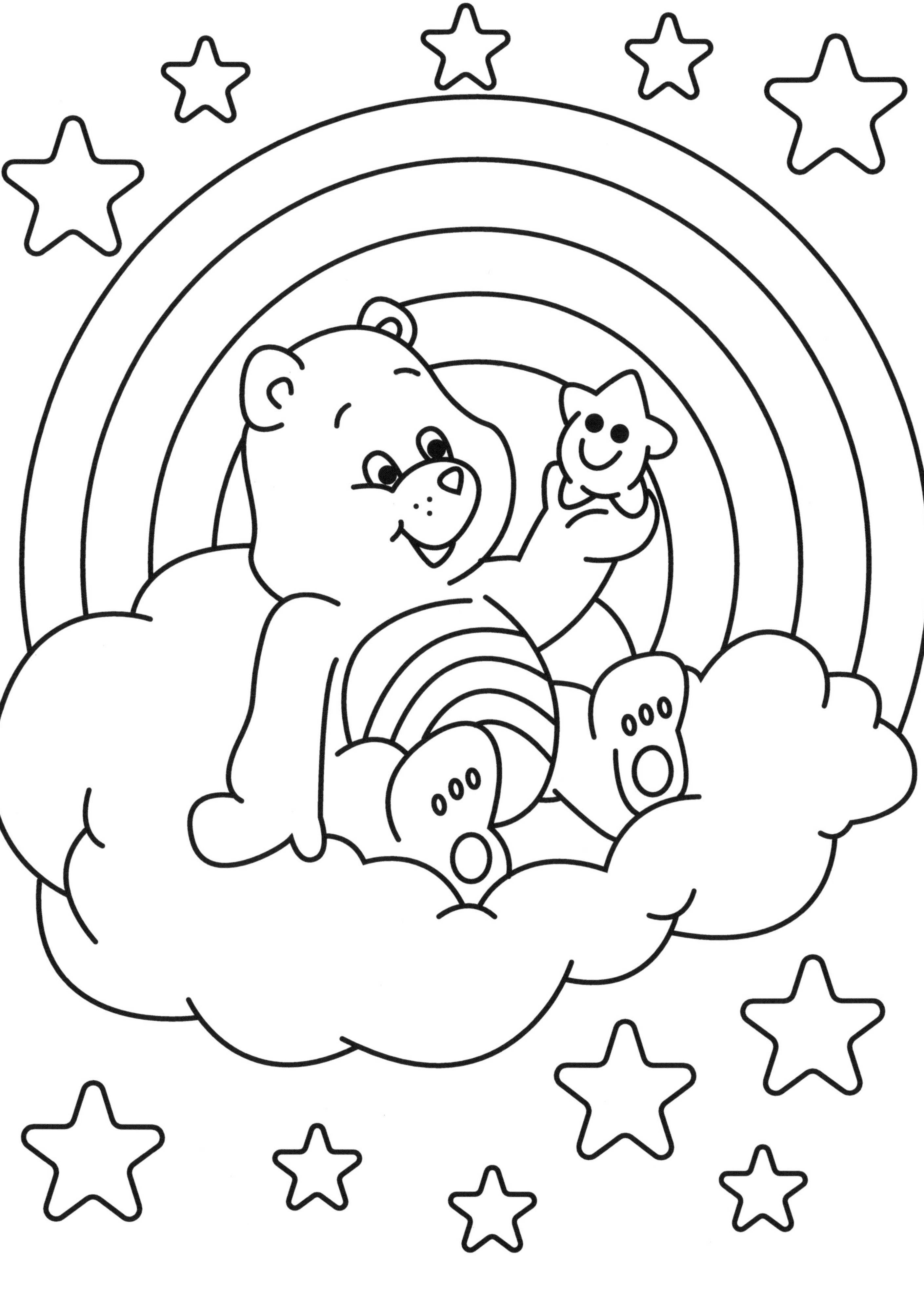

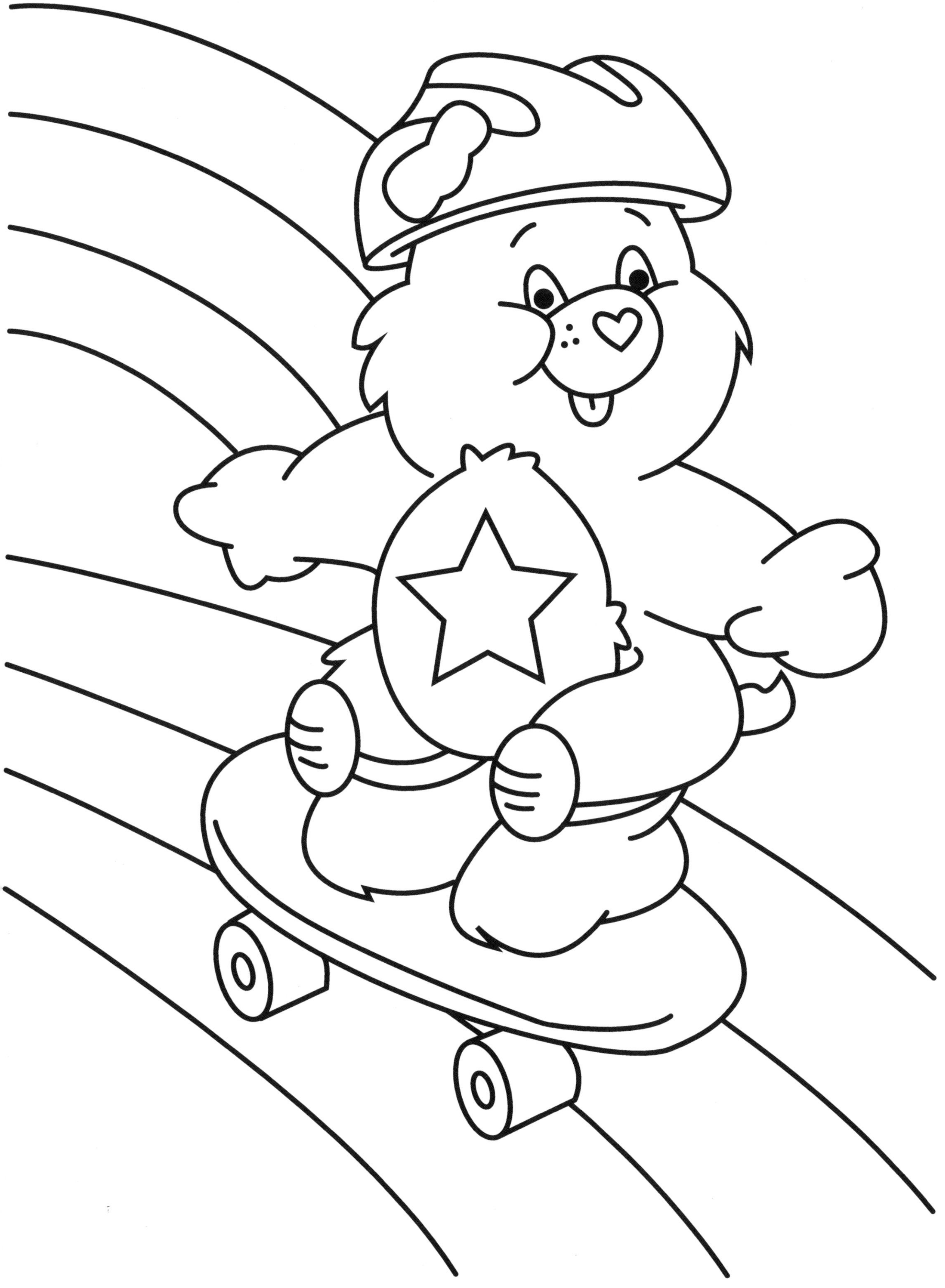

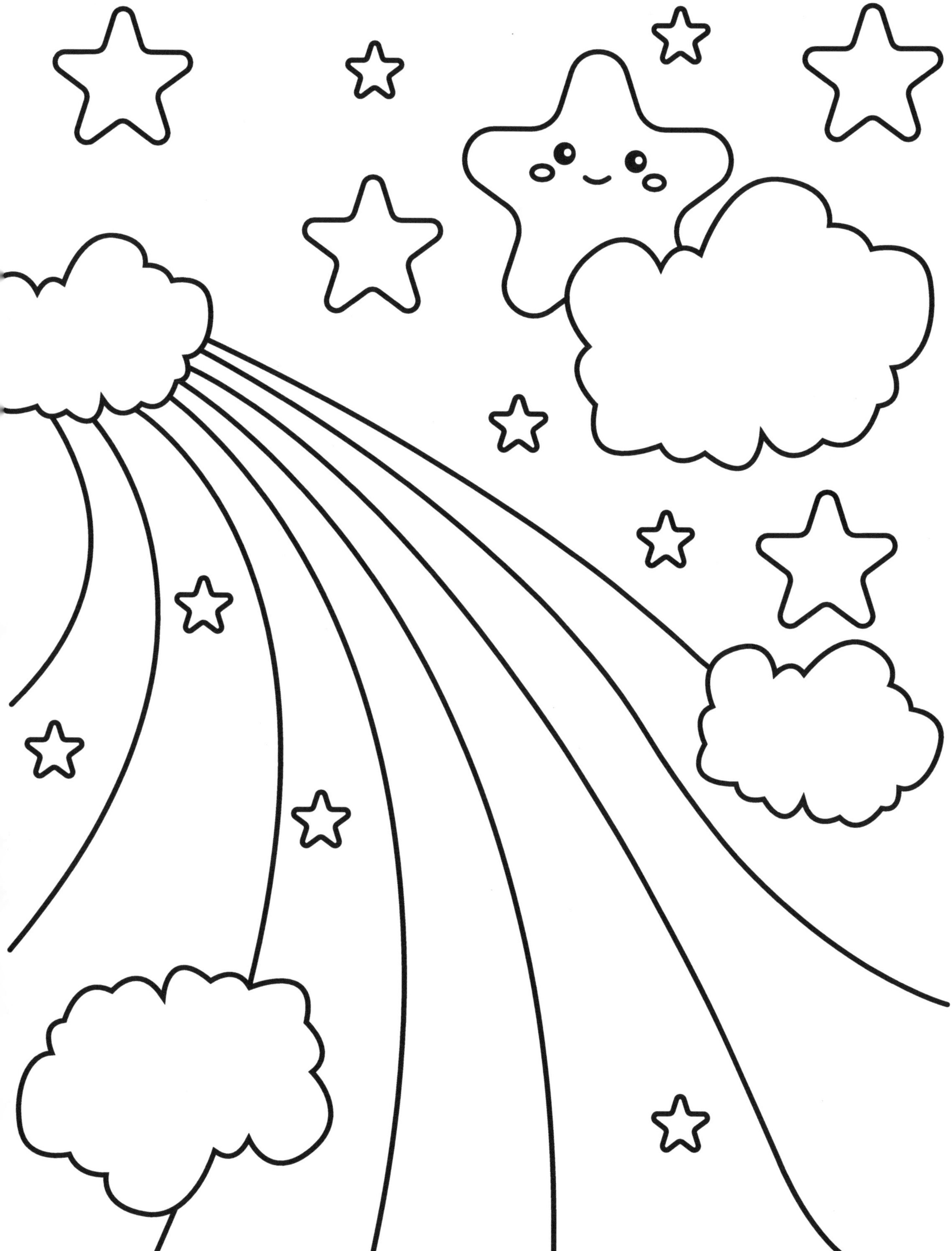

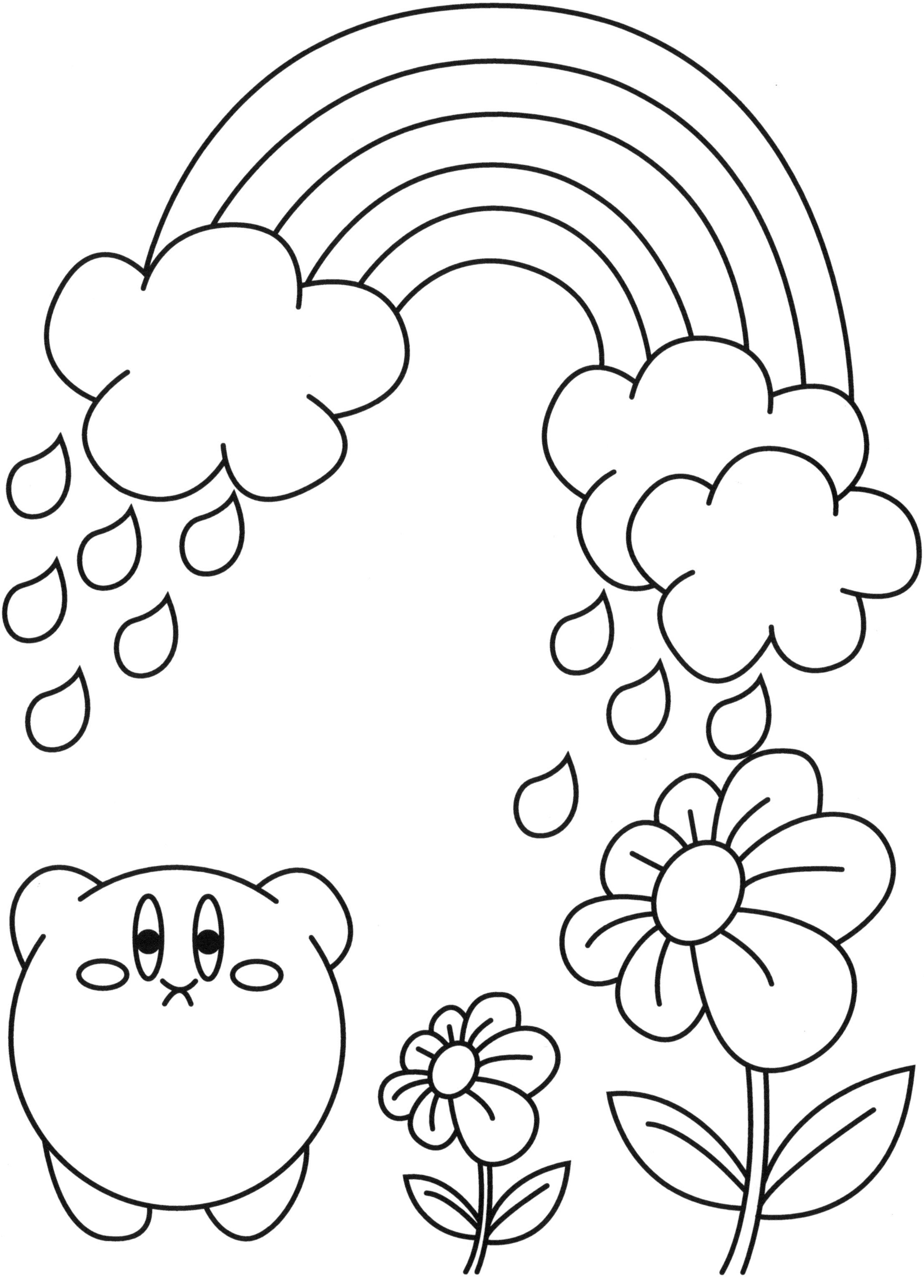

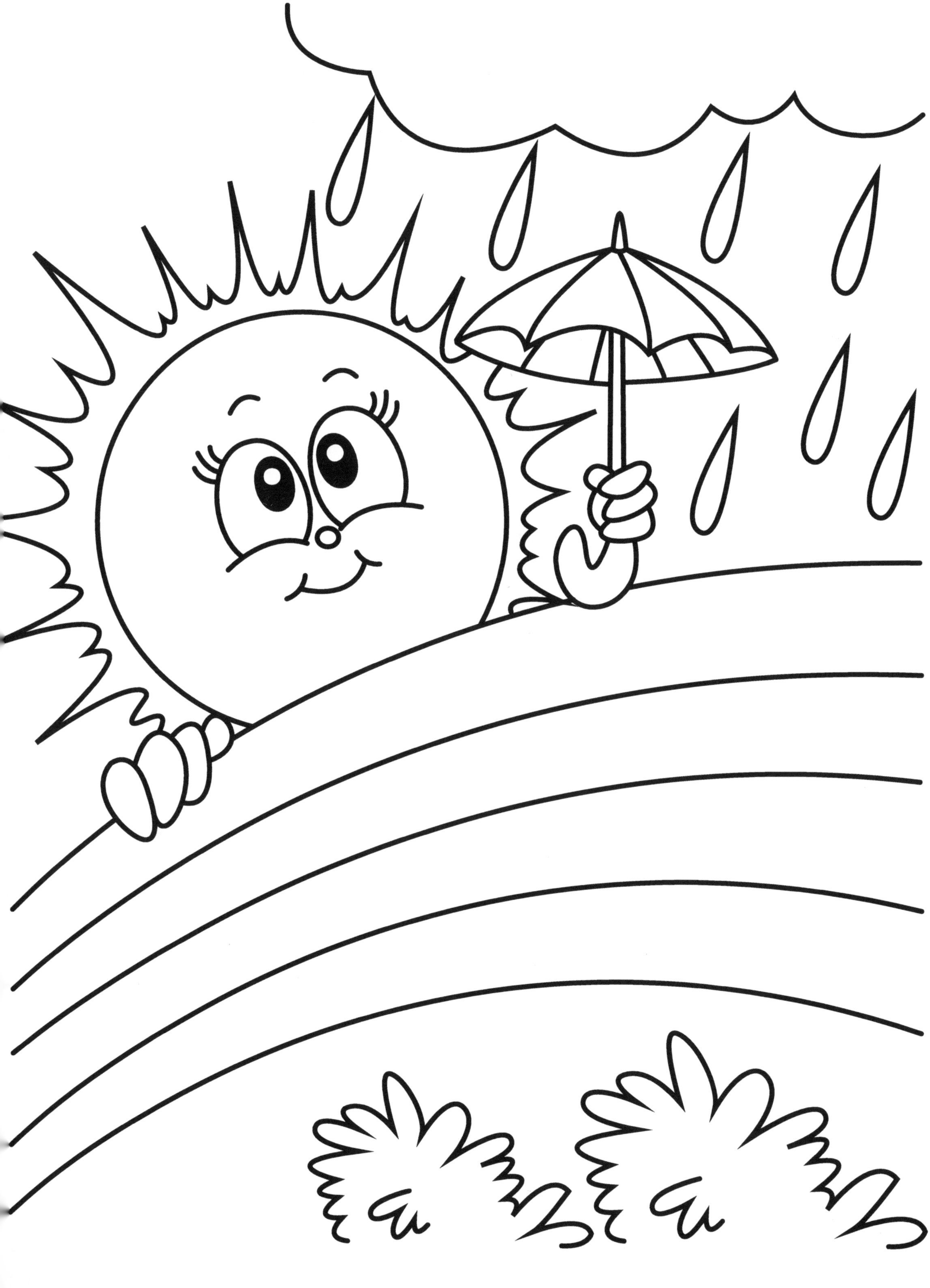

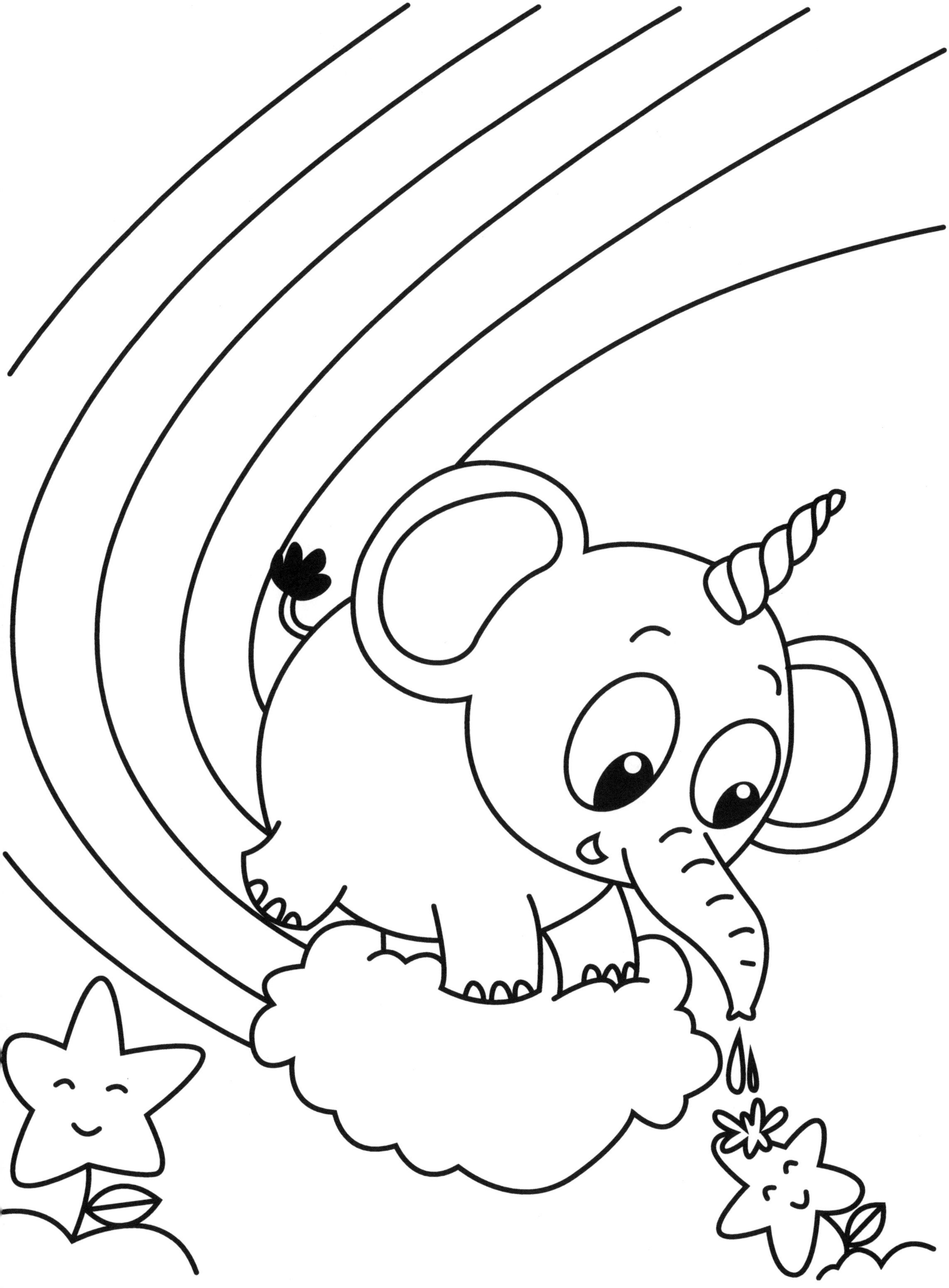

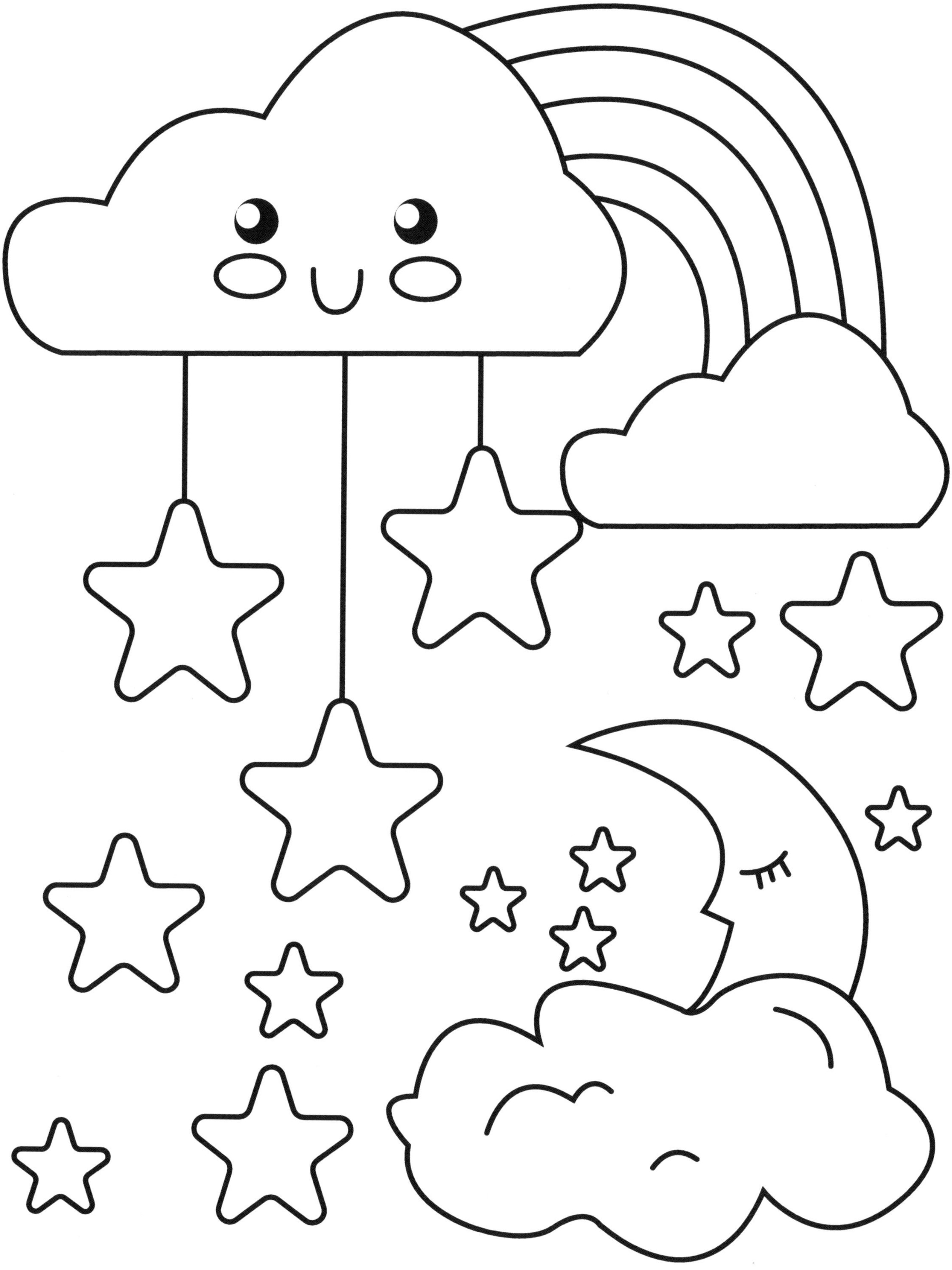

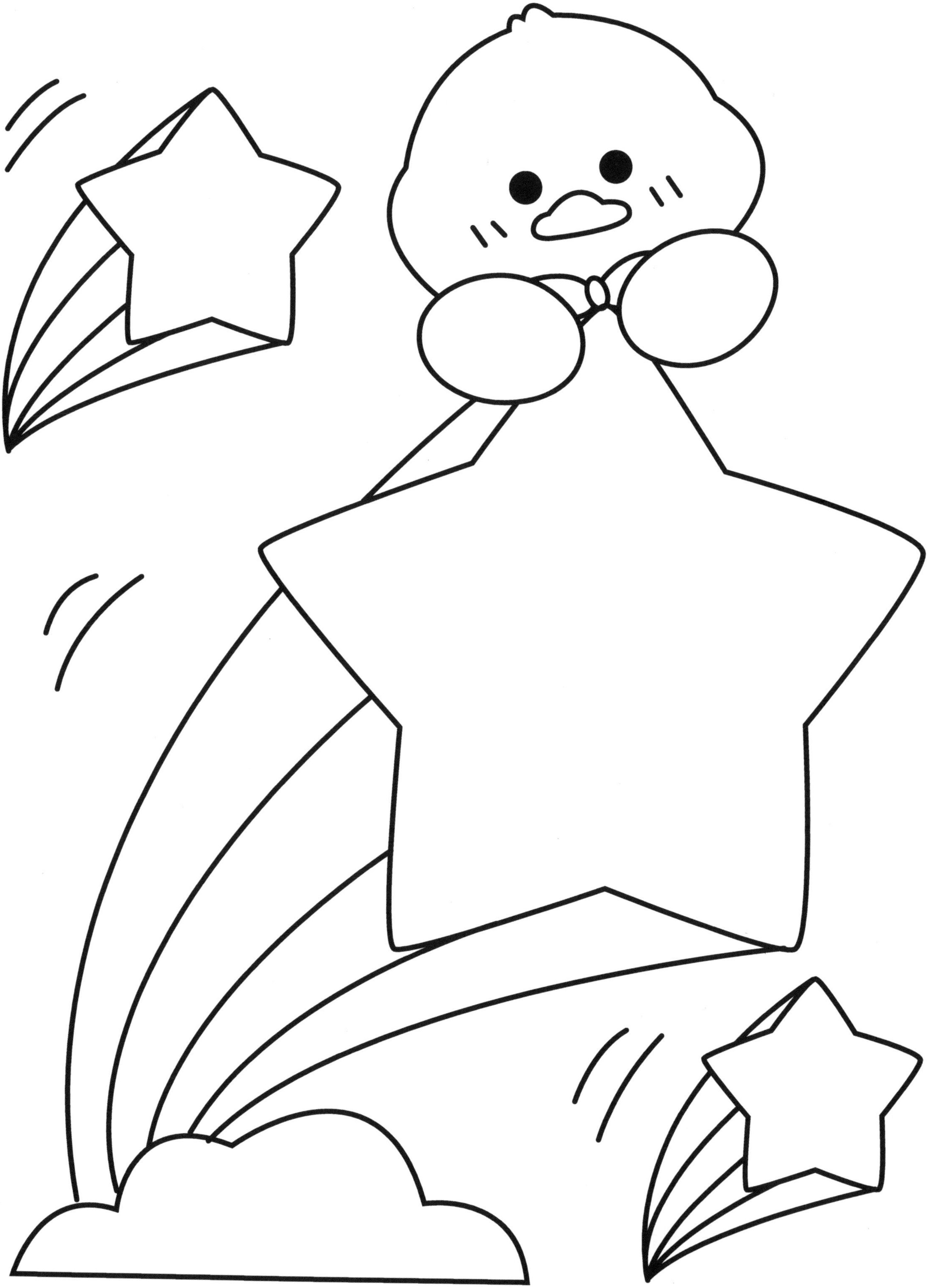

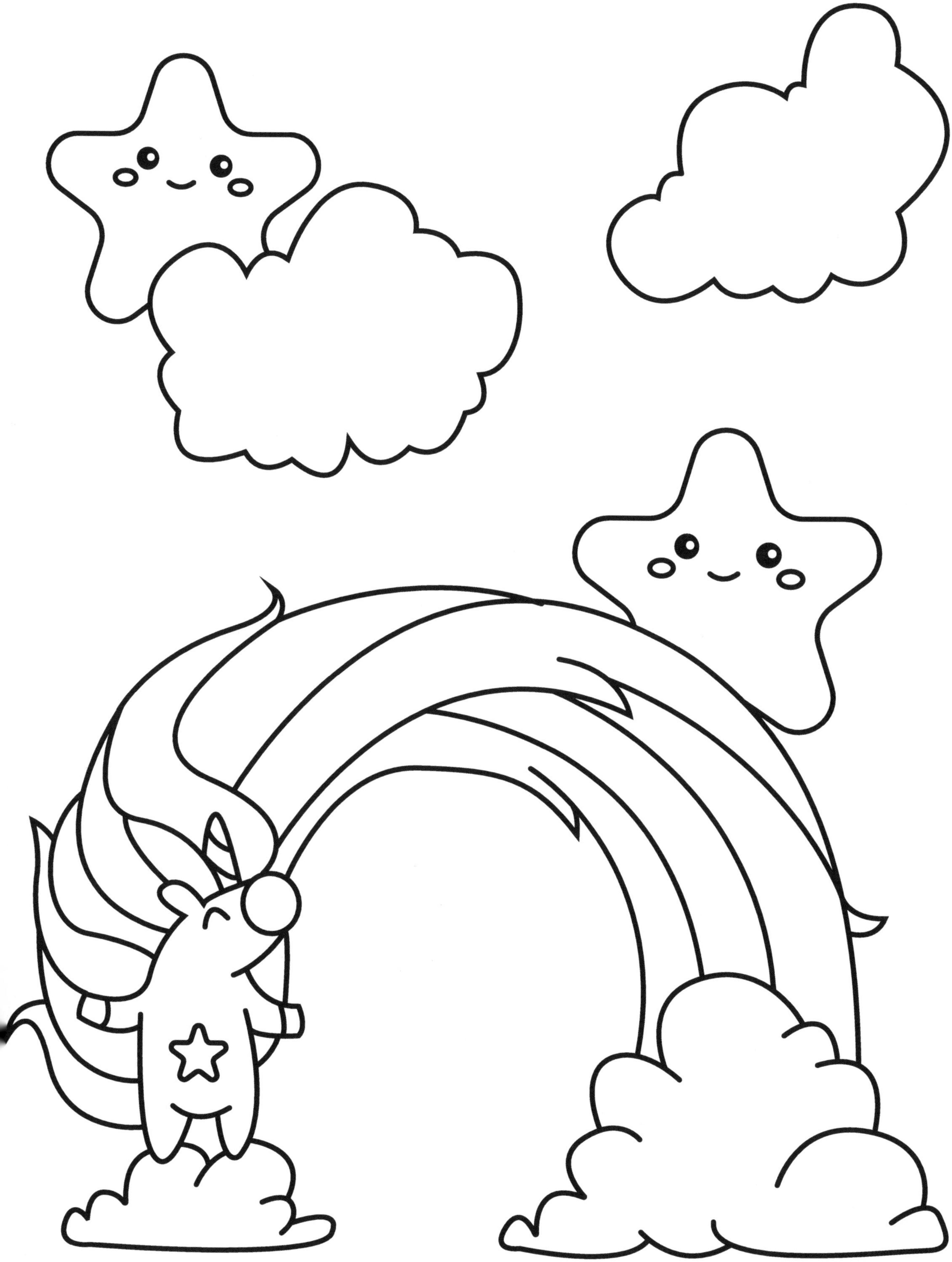

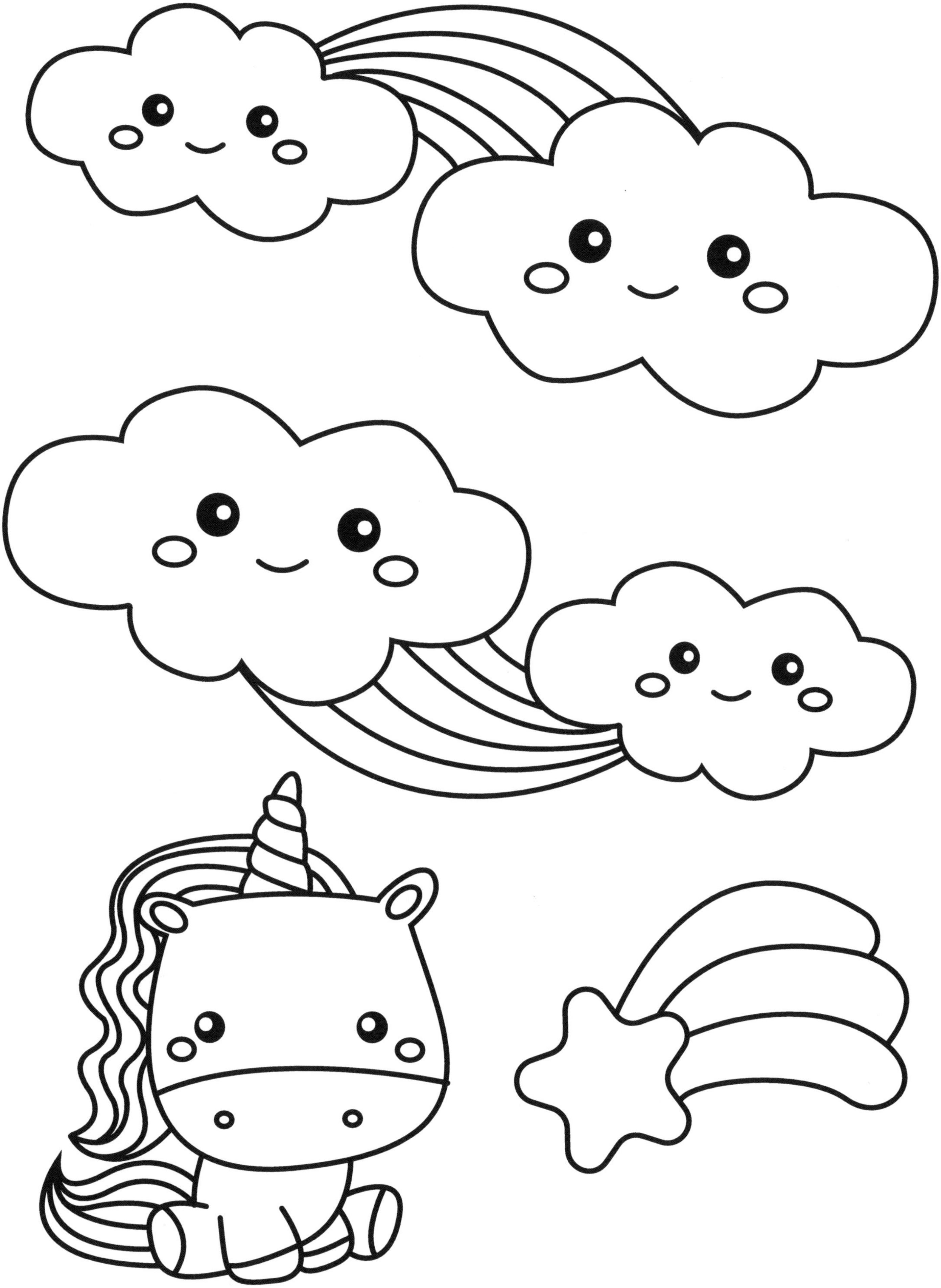

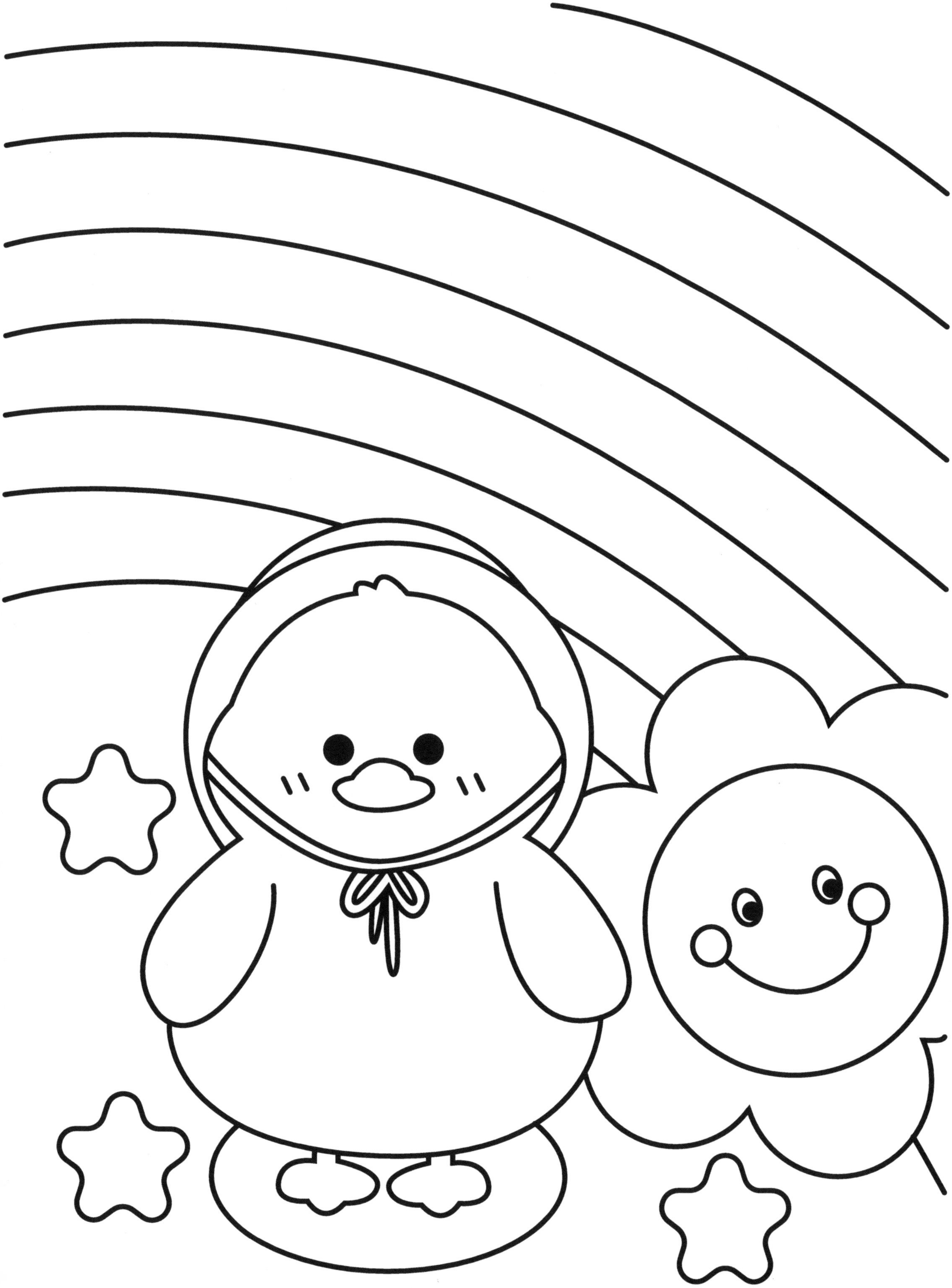

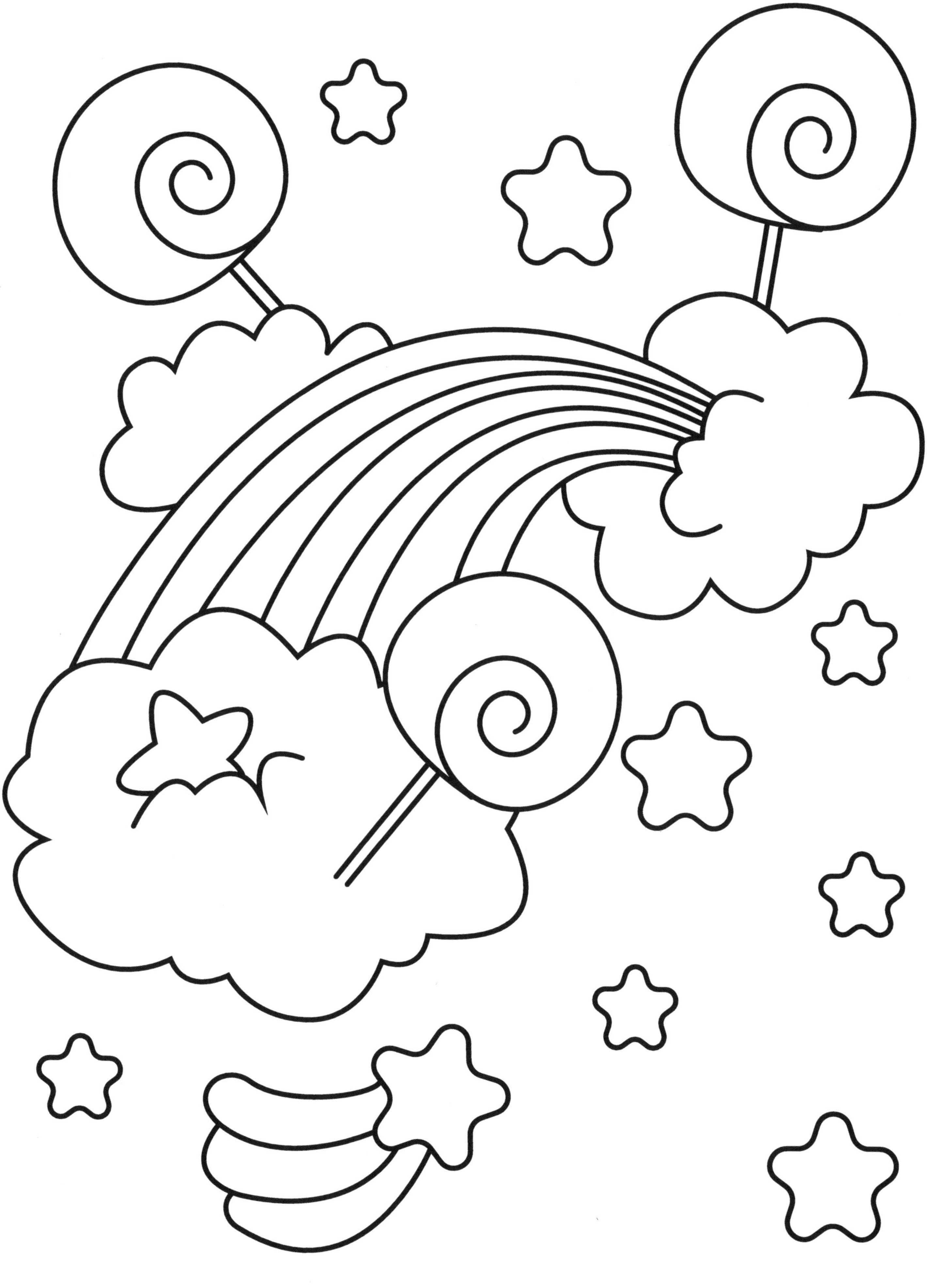

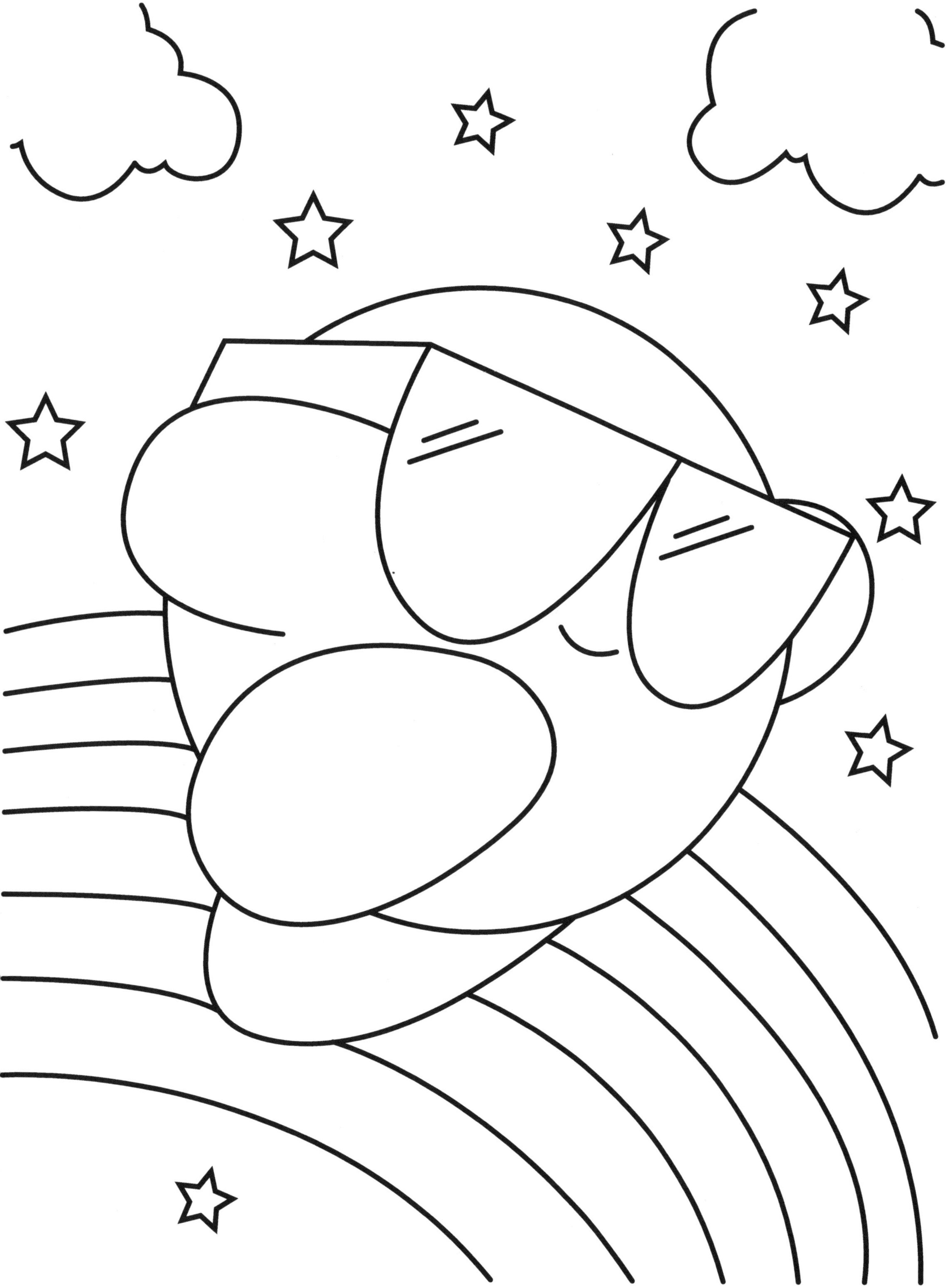

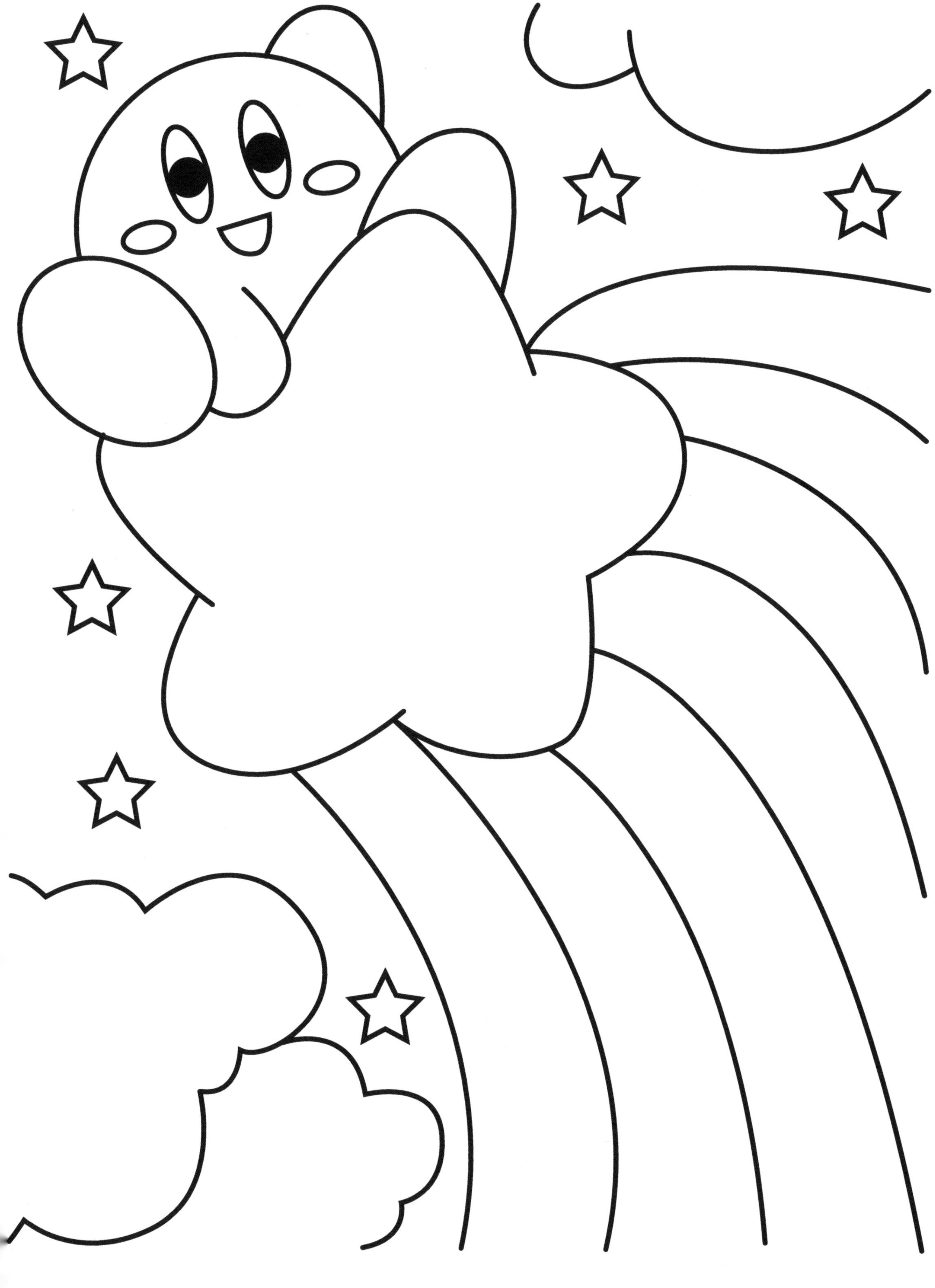

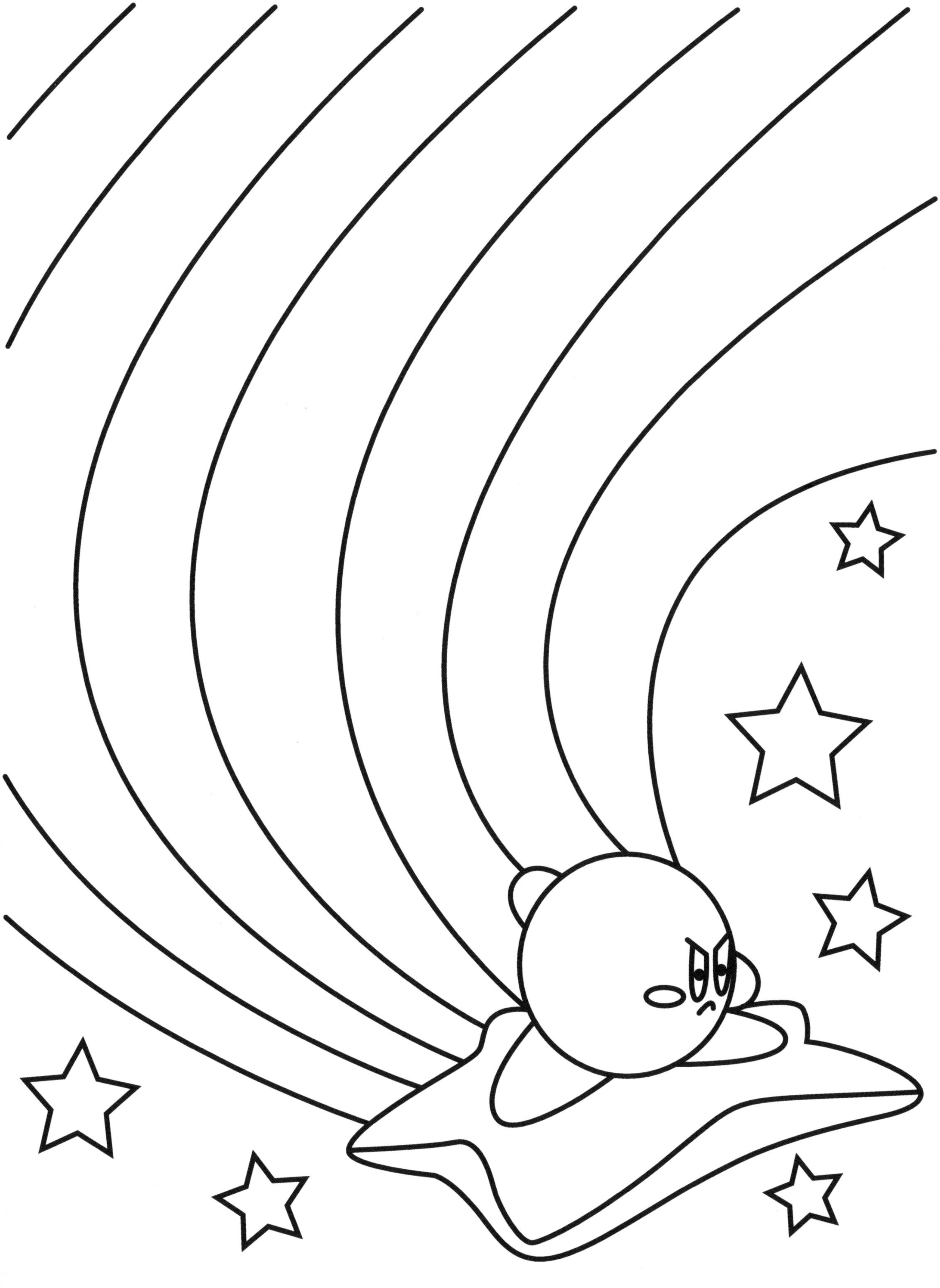

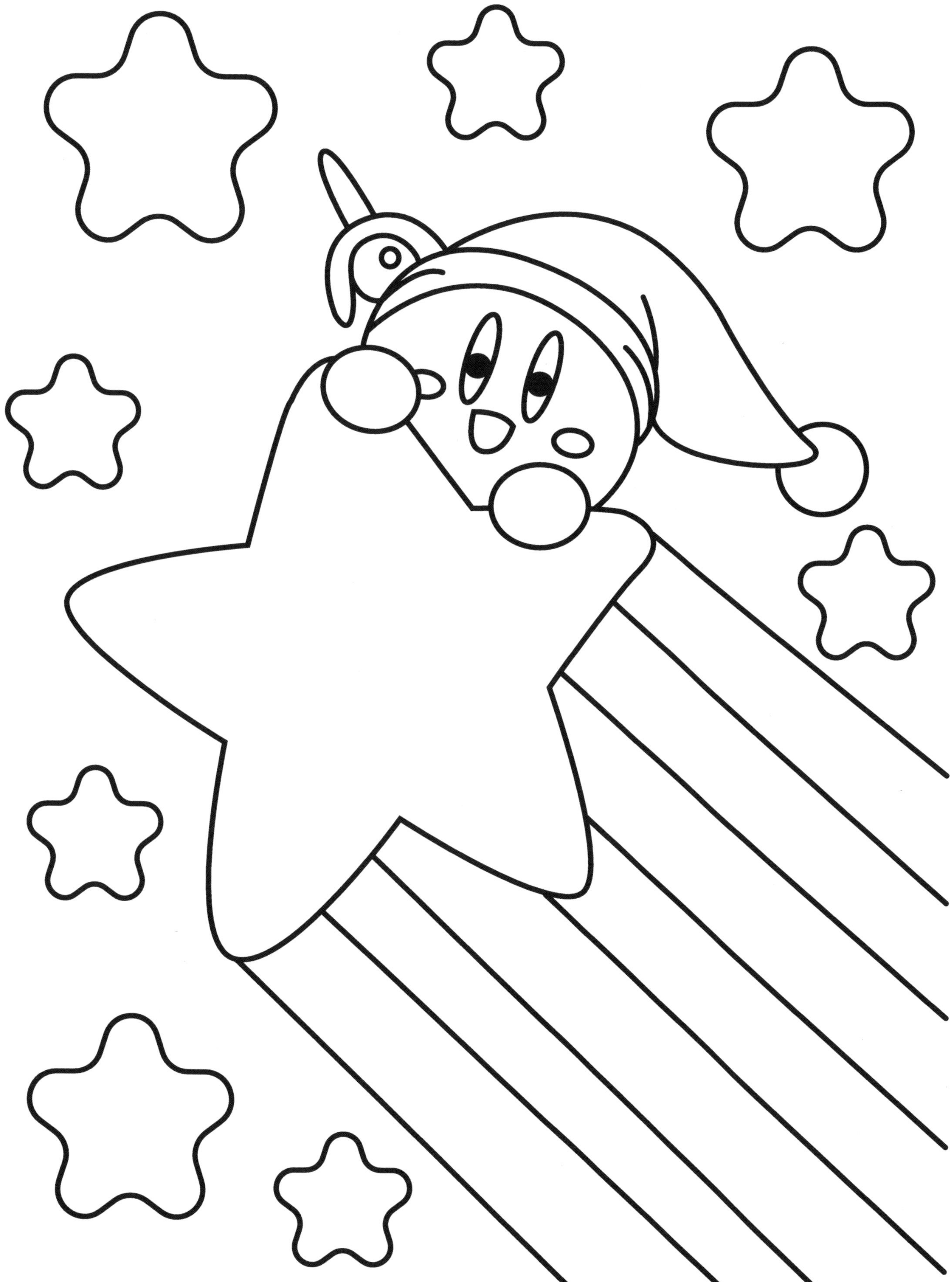

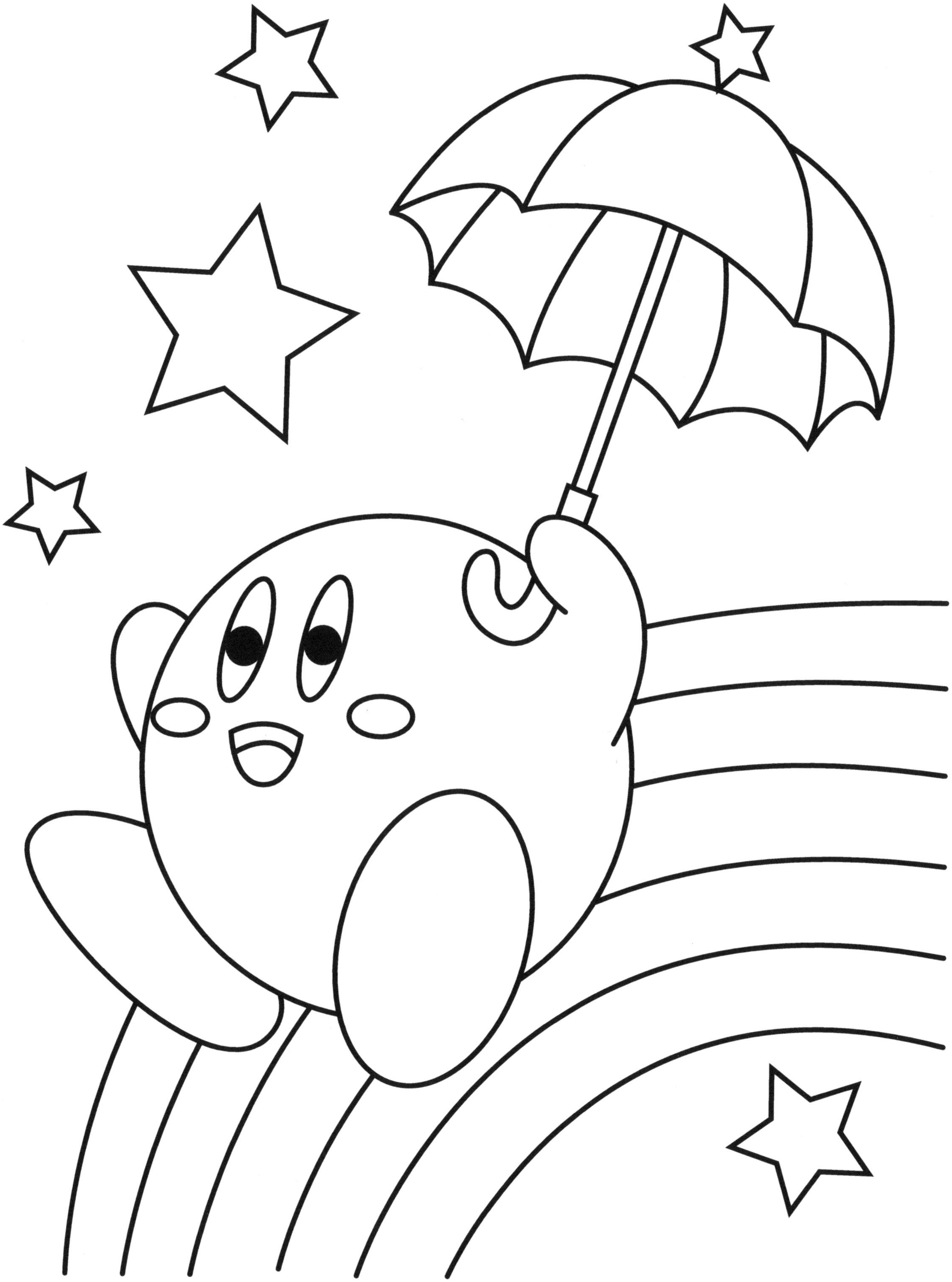

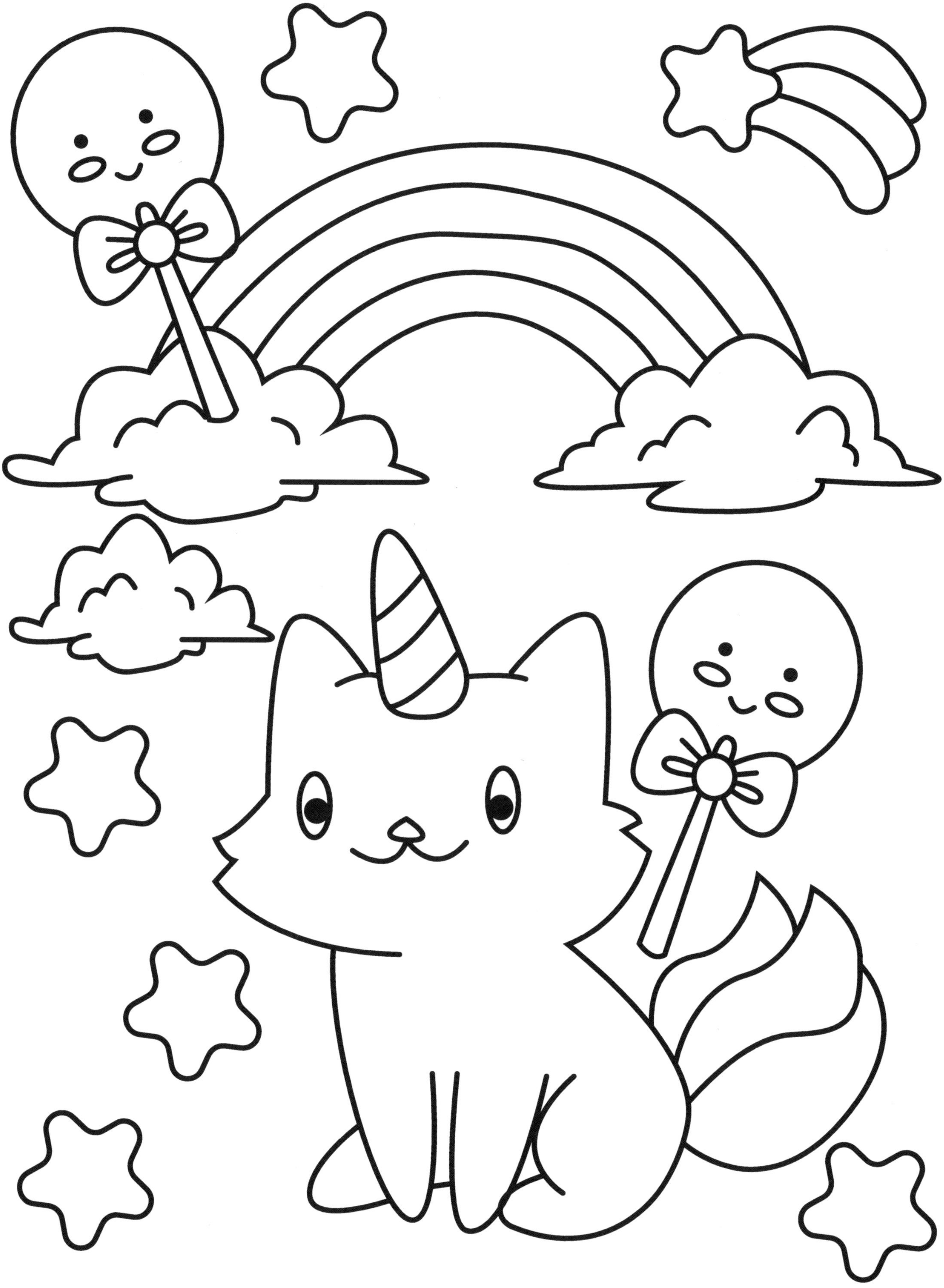

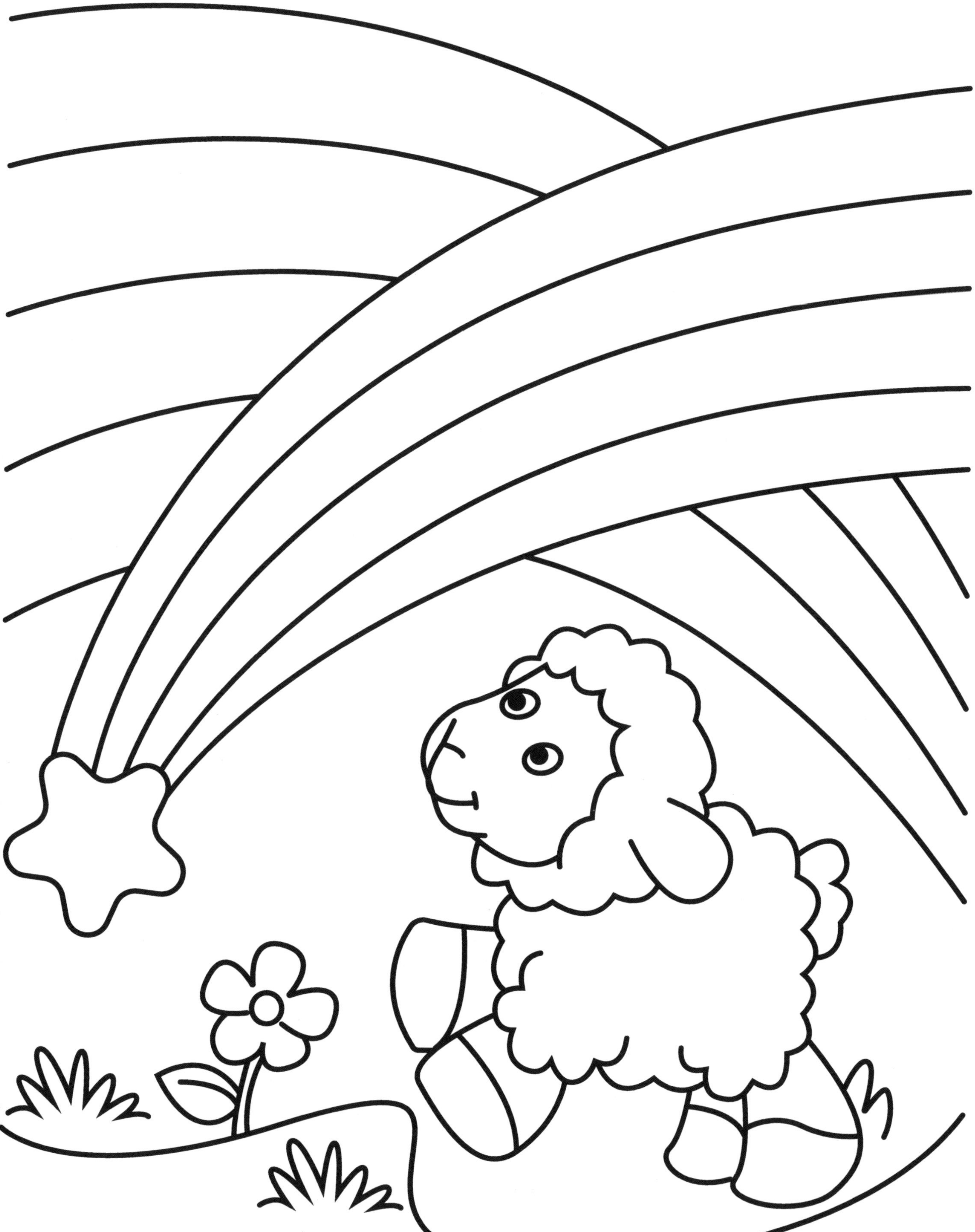

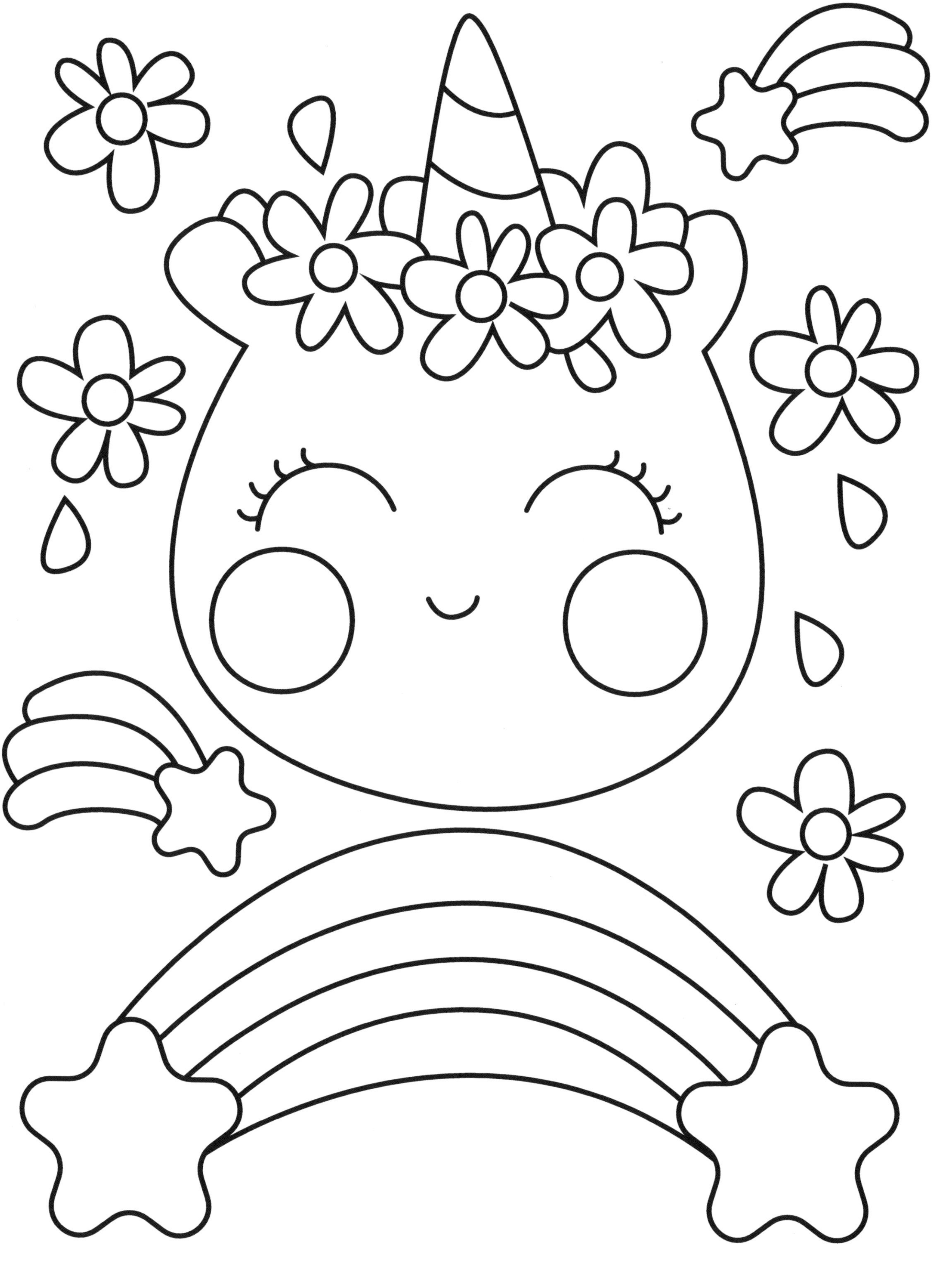

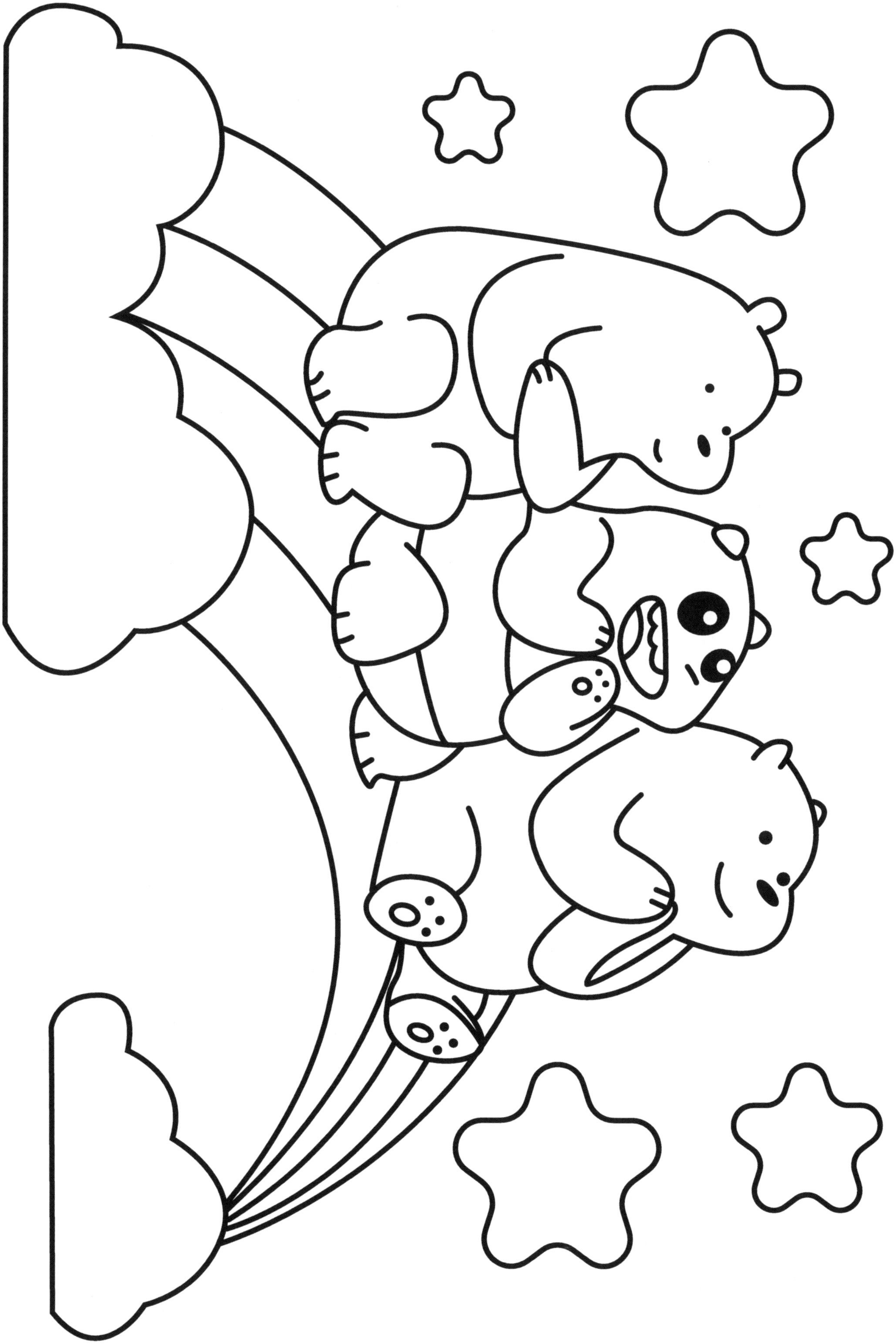

Made in the USA
Las Vegas, NV
14 December 2024

14223634R00061